SON OF ITALY

PICAS SERIES 36

PASCAL D'ANGELO

SON OF ITALY

AN AFTERWORD BY KENNETH SCAMBRAY

GUERNICA

TORONTO · BUFFALO · CHICAGO · LANCASTER (U.K.)

2003

Antonio D'Alfonso, editor
Guernica Editions Inc.
1569 Heritage Way, Oakville, (ON), Canada L6M 2Z7
2250 Military Road, Tonawanda, N.Y. 14150-6000 U.S.A.

Distributors:
University of Toronto Press Distribution,
5201 Dufferin Street, Toronto (ON), Canada M3H 5T8
Gazelle Book Services, White Cross Mills
High Town, Lancaster LA1 4XS U.K.

First edition by Guernica Editions.
Printed in Canada.

Legal Deposit — Second Quarter
National Library of Canada
Library of Congress Catalog Card Number: 2003105519
National Library of Canada Cataloguing in Publication
D'Angelo, Pascal, 1894
Son of Italy / Pascal D'Angelo. – 1st Guernica ed.
(Picas series ; 36)
First published under title: Pascal D'Angelo, son of Italy.
ISBN 1-55071-098-2

1. D'Angelo, Pascal, 1894-. 2. Italian Americans – Biography.
3. Padrone system. I. Title. II. Series.
E184.I8 D35 2002   331.6'245073 C2002-905351-X

This book is dedicated to Mr. Luigi Forgione whose aid and encouragement have made its appearance possible. The author is indebted to the following magazines and newspapers: *Literary Review, The Liberator, The Bookman, The Measure, The Nation,* and *Il Popolo* and *Bollettino della sera* for permission to republish the poems found in this volume.

CHAPTER I

As I glance back over the time-shadowed sky of my infancy, I seem to see a vast expanse of mist that gives no light to any early events. But here and there looms a faint pyramid of recollection that can apparently never fade. Toward them I grope, almost in a twilight of memory, seeking to bring out what really happened to me while I passed through the little world of inevitable childhood and poverty. My first real recollection probably runs down to a little less than four years – for my grandmother died then. And I clearly remember when she made me go up to the garret to get onions in order to have them roasted under hot cinders of the wood fire that we used in place of a stove. It undoubtedly must have been winter, for it is in winter that such things are properly in use.

She said, "Get the onions from under the bed, and we will roast and eat them."

So I began to climb the stepladder, hesitating. She climbed half the way up speaking words of encouragement. One of the chief causes for my fear at that time was that the garret had no window and the only light that came in was what penetrated through the cracks of the tile roof. I was also frightened at the horrible dragging noise of a caravan of enormous rats that promenaded back and forth along the roof under the hollow spaces of the clay tiles, our house being a "catless" house.

This garret was divided in two unequal parts. The largest in front where the roof descended very low was filled with firewood. In the small center part was the bed on which my mother, my father, my brother and I slept. A very narrow bed it was. Almost every night I fell, having my head continually decorated with swollen spots about the size of a full ripe cherry. The reason for these falls was my being laid asleep beneath my mother's and father's feet, because I was bigger than my brother and therefore could better guard myself. My brother was two years younger than I. He lay between them while they slept uncomfortably on either side as if margining the space of his safety. As I slept crosswise beneath their feet they could never stretch their legs, for whenever they did so they felt my little body and immediately shrank back frightened lest they push me off the bed. In spite of my few years, I sometimes could not sleep for lack of sufficient room. But when my parents got up to go to work, I could choose a better place, I and my brother being left on the bed to sleep all we wished.

One night – I really do not know what time it was, nor do I suppose my father knew, for poverty prevented our having a watch – I suddenly awoke with a cry. It may have been during the dread-tangled midnight hours. A heavy patter of down-pouring rain was sweeping the rustic tile roof above our heads.

It was the frequent and heavy drops of rain falling on my face that awoke me.

Immediately I found myself up, and my awakened parents were putting a heavy deep clay plate on my sleeping place. I was shivering. But my mother gathered all her dresses and petticoats and put them on the floor, making a little bed for me to pass the unknown remainder of the night.

In the lower part of the house was a general living room, kitchen and dining room. At night it was the sleeping place for the animals – the goats and sheep which we were lucky enough to own.

Another time, probably much earlier than this, a child who was playing with me fell down – I don't know how – and began to cry. Madly its mother hurried toward us as if I had been the cause of her child's fall. As I saw her shriekingly approach me I tried to run away, but entangled in the threads of slow infancy, I could not. I felt her huge rage-gripping hand that caught my loosely buttoned dress. Weeping I told her that I hadn't done anything to her child.

Promptly she said, "Then why are you running away?"

I didn't know what to answer at first; but my fright gave me the ability to say, "Ask your child if I made him fall."

In answer she tried to catch me by the ears and drag me back to where her son was pleasantly crying. I cried, "What do you think I am, a rabbit, that you bring me by the ears?"

Anyhow, she brought me in front of her child. Fortunately for me the boy told the truth; which is a rare thing. Otherwise I would have received a few healthy slaps that she had prepared for me.

She answered that I was dismissed, and I went away solemnly thinking, "Wait till I grow bigger. Then if something happens I can courageously run away." But that's a thing I never did save once much later when I was about six or seven.

At that time I found myself in front of my uncle's house together with two other boys one of them three years older and the other about five months younger than I. In this case the cause is not as evident to my memory as the effect. Whatever it was, the bigger boy threw the younger one on the ground, and then putting a stone in my little hand told me to hit him. I had no reason to do so, and even if I had I would have not done it, for ferocity has never been able to develop within me.

The big boy had the younger lad pressed against the solid ground in front of my relatives' house. All of a sudden I didn't have the stone in my hand. Whether I threw it on the ground, or whether it fell out of my hand, I don't know.

Blood was coming from the fallen boy's head and the bigger boy was shouting that I did it. It was sometime before noon. The small boy began to toddle crying toward his house with a few drops of blood gleaming on his forehead. And I – where could I go? My father wouldn't defend me if his father came into my house to hit me, nor my mother if his mother came into my house and hit me. What my parents always told me was, "When you know that they are like that why do you go with them?"

So I could not go home because I had no protection there. Neither could I stay where I was, for the boy's mother would soon be coming out to beat me.

It would have been a good thing not to run away. But the boys, especially the younger, were insisting that I had made the wound and they would tell his people.

What I had to do, I thought, was to avoid the first storm of rage that his mother could cast upon me. I set myself walking hurriedly across the cultivated fields in order to find shelter or a hiding place. It was very hard to go across a vast stretch of freshly tilled land because my feet sank deep at every step. Amid the many various fields I was unable to find a safe refuge. Not too far away a provincial highway passes by with several little bridges. I chose the nearest one of them, under which no water was running. And there I hid under the low dark arch. Every now and then I peeked out to see if someone were coming toward me. I knew that I could easily be entrapped in that long narrow tunnel. I was afraid. Suppose someone had seen me and had told the boy's mother that if she wanted me I could be found under the bridge?

As I was glancing out, around a curve of the road, not far away from me loomed the figure of a large girl. She had ten or fifteen sheep and lambs before her and was slowly pasturing them on the sides of the broad, grass-shouldered road. Headlong I scampered back into the moist manmade den. I stood there thinking, confused, when a rough shout startled me.

"What are you doing there?"

All frightened I felt myself already caught. Hesitating, I went outward. I heard a lamb bleating up the road, and I felt a little hope that she might just be a passing shepherdess, and not someone from the village seeking me.

I went out with a peculiar expression on my face such as I had never had before, one of forced innocence. Once out on the road I recognized her as that boy's sister.

Curiously she asked me why I was hiding in there. She did not appear to know what had happened, probably having been out with her sheep and lambs all day long.

Her presence seemed like a storm before me – those storms that madly seize the placid silence of our valley. I trembled in front of her.

She was older than I. Therefore I moved away slowly at first. Her eyes followed me in astonishment. And then at a good distance I shouted out to her what they accused me of.

"No!" she answered with an incredulous air, "it's not true. It cannot be. I don't believe it."

"Well," I answered, a little assured and moving nearer, "I myself don't believe it either, but the others do."

She hesitated a moment. She really thought I was

joking with her and seemed decided to show that I couldn't fool her.

So, after a little silence she laughed in that skeptic way that the people of our valley have.

And shaking her head she went on, pasturing her sheep slowly and gradually disappearing beyond the hiding curve of the broad road.

Now and then I could hear the bleating of the lambs in the distance. Finally these sounds ceased and the countryside became still and serene as before.

I descended the green escarpment and, having no better place to go, went back under the little narrow bridge, fully dominated by fear. I probably must have wept a little, too. Gradually, while weeping, I abandoned myself upon the soothing bosom of dreams. And I slept, or just half-slept. I even forgot that I had not eaten which is a child's principal concern. Perhaps all was well.

Now and then a horse wagon went rumbling by, like a harsh note in my vague dreams. Braying asses went past and their sounds spread lazily across the vast green of the crop-laden fields. I dreamed.

At first my dreams were vain infantile fancies, little fallacies that the mind of a child can sketch on the pallor of vision. But gradually a great struggle awoke in my dream. I was climbing a hard monstrous mountain, I did not know why. It was vaster and more tremendous than our glorious Majella, the mother mountain. I did not know why I struggled so hard, but I was being urged onward – an awakened spirit in me was yearning to reach the top. Finally, after a long time I found myself on the highest heaven-touching peak of this mystic enormity. A tree, soft and green glowed up there with a tempting nest filled with the most beautiful birds that I could ever imagine. I climbed. The mountain below caved in. The branch that I clung to broke. And down I fell, down, down, forever.

With a start I awoke. I was frightened. Young though I was I felt the presence of something invisible yet existent, which had shown itself in my dream.

We of the uplands of Abruzzi are a different race. The inhabitants of the soft plains of Latium and Apulia where in winter we pasture our sheep consider us a people of seers and poets. We believe in dreams. There are strange beings walking through our towns whose existence, we know, are phantasies. We have men who can tell the future and ageless hags who know the secrets of the mountain and can cure all illness save witchcraft with a few words.

As I crouched there in fright I felt a tremor in the air. A volume of wind came pouring through the tunnel. A stream came trickling through. I heard the rain beating down. Lightning flashed around. The volume of the torrent under the bridge was increasing with every second. Out into the storm I ran, caring only to reach home. Immediately I was wet to the skin. It was impossible to go across the glistening, soggy fields. I had to follow the road, which was a long round-about way.

Hunger possessed me. Home seemed very desirable. I began to cry while trudging on. It was getting dark.

By that time the boy's sister must have reached the hamlet and told her parents about me. They were probably watching from their stone house for my return. Little by little the rainfall ceased, and a pouring night wiped all the rosy stains of twilight from the tattered clouds. As I hesitated, I could see, far below me the little cluster of houses that formed our hamlet, pale against the black gleaming fields. The smoke from these houses rose upward in twisting colonnades and blent with the wild infinity of night. A light appeared at one window. And still I hesitated, fearing to approach my home.

Finally, little by little, I drew near. Members of the boy's family were outside the house, some were at their windows. I heard someone shouting my name. And I knew that they were searching for me.

Well, were my thoughts, it's not a murder I have committed, so I might as well approach and hear their shrieking preludes. If these are extremely unpleasant and threatening, I can easily vanish again into the night.

Making a show of bravery, I marched decisively onward. I would hardly be safe in my own house, for they would come in and beat me there. Being older and practically relatives they had the right to do that, and my father would not think of stopping them.

As I approached, trembling, I heard my mother's soothing voice calling my name and saying that there was no serious trouble, only a little scratch the child must have received when the big boy threw him down.

Instinctively I sobbed out, like a lamb that answers the bleating call of its mother.

I ran on. Soon I reached the half-broken three steps that led up to my house. As I was on the second step I felt a rough hand grab my shoulder and lips shouting in my ear.

I trembled and howled. My mother's voice uttered sharply, "Let him go! You know he has done nothing."

It was that boy's oldest brother who had caught me and had shouted to frighten me, probably as a compensation for what I had been accused of doing to his brother.

Sullenly the tall young man answered, "Don't be afraid, I am only fooling." And to me, "You didn't do anything to him, otherwise I would have searched you out no matter where you had hidden."

Overjoyed, with assured innocence, I entered the house in one leap.

And my mother smiled after me.

CHAPTER II

The hamlet where I was born on January 20, 1894, is comprised of a small group of stone houses near Introdacqua and not very far from the old walled city of Sulmona. Introdacqua nestles at the head of a beautiful valley whose soft green is walled in by the great blue barrens of Monte Majella. The mother mountain looms to the east of us and receives the full splendor of the dawn. We are proud to call ourselves the sons of the majestic Majella. And our race, the ancient Samnites, is said to have sprung from those sunny altitudes and spread their power over all Italy, making even Rome tremble.

Few roads run to this quiet land and the old traditions have never entirely died out there. Below the town is the garden of Ovid with wild roses and cool springs, and above is an ancient castle that in summer is fantastically crowned with mingling flights of wild pigeons that take care of their younglings on its towered heights. In the valley beyond are finely cultivated fields dotted with the ruins of Italica, the capital of fierce Samnium.

One day, when I was about six, my mother had to go to the town, which was a little more than "half an hour's walk" away. Childishly, I insisted on going with her.

Unsuccessfully my mother tried to keep down the tiny folly that had intruded into my young mind. I began to wail and cry. She made many promises that are wonderful to children and can only be told to them. I wanted to go.

She told me that the town was too far – Oh! very far – that I would get tired before we reached half way.

"It's not far," I insisted, "we can hear the bells when it gets dark."

"But the bells are placed away up high on the church tower," she explained. I refused to understand.

She continued, "Just because the sound reaches us doesn't mean that they are near. Look – the water comes here, too, passing by our neighbor's house. And see what a distance it comes from," pointing with her finger toward where the peaks of the azure mountain were barely visible in a mist of heights with their red rifts that seemed to be the unhealed scars left by the storms that rage up there. Only a ruddy cloud was kinging the softened blue above them.

As she spoke I saw my mother's eyes gaze anxiously at that cloud hovering over the mountain. At that time she seemed to be the most beautiful woman in the world to me, though I now realize how care and hard work had given her face a thoughtful expression.

However, we set out. I walked ahead as fast as I could and she sauntered slowly with me. We had hardly gone a few minutes when something seemed to have blurred the sun. Again my mother looked around. The sky was no longer clear blue, but had a pale misty color. We hurried on, that is, I walked as fast as I could and she followed me.

Now, in a few minutes a darkness settled upon the valley. It seemed as if it closed in from every side. And thunder rumbled. My mother looked around. I became frightened. Lightning tore across the sky over the mountain. And all at once the rain came flooding down. Quickly my mother picked me up and ran for a small stone hut nearby. As she approached through the twisting curtain of rain two savage dogs dashed out toward us. They had their heads low and mouths open, growling evilly. I cried in fear. My mother stopped and in a sharp voice called out. Someone whistled. The dogs stopped short. An old man appeared at the door of the hut and stared at us through the wild rain. On either side of the house were two tall scrawny trees with their lower branches cut off to prevent a shadow from hurting the crops below.

This man had been known as a sort of wizard.

He lived alone and had little to do with the world. He seemed to hate all who came near him. He cried in a harsh voice, "What do you want?"

"Shelter."

He laughed and called back his dogs. Just then the two trees alongside the hut became tipped with flame and something like a great star appeared in the doorway over the man's head. And a terrific thun-

der broke upon us. The man fell. The lightning had
blinded us all for an instant. Then my mother, who
still gripped me in her arms, shrieked and began to
run down the road. Down, toward the town, through
the rain, dashing through pools of water she fled.
At the first houses some of the people came out and
helped her in. I was wondering.

My mother, hysterically, cried out the news that
the old man had been struck by the fires of heaven.
Out rushed the men, through the rain which was
increasing every minute. After a short while they came
back, all wet, and sadly announced that he was dead.
Everybody seemed dazed. Meanwhile, the storm was
tearing across our valley. Great whirls of shining rain
were swaying about. The house shook as the thunder crashed nearby. And I had begun to get acquainted
with a boy in the house and we were sitting on the
floor playing with walnuts that we had taken from
a box.

This was the first really tragic incident in my life
and it made a profound impression upon me, not
so much at that time as later in my memory.

Introdacqua is a beautiful town and nature ap-
pears to have squandered beauty on the surrounding vistas. The people are very quiet and extremely
peaceful.

When good seasons are with us the valley is happy
and the sturdy peasants walk jovially to work in the
early morning, and sing in harmony with the heaven-
soaring larks. But when the years are bad and the
dreaded droughts hover over the land they are silent

and one sees sorrow, care and even hunger in their eyes.

But one good season will make them happy again. And in the evenings after a hard day's toil, they will stay out late in the moonlight when the nightingales sing. And in spite of having heard them so often, these peasants' interest and desire to hear them again seems to be ceaseless.

But we, the young ones, had a mania for birds' nests rather than their songs. And we were always prowling through the neighboring fields, in groups, seeking them. Up we climbed, up apple trees, cherry trees, almond trees, and in short, up any place on which a little nest might be perched. In the spring when everything is in flower and tender we caused quite a little damage.

Inevitably after these expeditions, on reaching home, we received beatings from our parents. But we didn't care. And sometimes, after the whippings we would get together in the home of one of us and talk. Then one would try to show how brave he would have been in case we had found a nest upon some tree whose trunk and branches were crowded with coils of freshly budded grape vines. This was the sole thing we had any respect for, and experience had taught us that any depredation committed on the grape vines would be severely punished. First we had to deal with the owner if he had good eyes to see us and good legs to catch us; but more certain was the punishment of our parents who on learning of our misdeed would beat us severely. And there was no escaping our fathers either. But my boyhood was not all play, and very early I knew what work was.

Still there were dreams for me. A poem of mine which was printed long afterwards may perhaps give an idea of the region and light surrounding me:

MIDDAY

The road is like a little child running ahead of
me and then hiding behind a curve –
Perhaps to surprise me when I reach there.
The sun has built a nest of light under the eaves of
noon;
A lark drops down from the cloudless sky
Like a singing arrow, wet with blue, sped from the
bow of space.
But my eyes pierce the soft azure, far, far beyond,
To where roam eternal lovers
Along the broad blue ways
Of silence.

I was sent to school at the age of seven. It was a small place kept by a gentle voiced lady. My attendance was very irregular, for I was the first boy of the family big enough to help my parents. My father had five or six sheep and four goats and I had to watch them – not because he wanted to prevent my going to school, but because he could not afford to hire an older boy. In spite of my frequent absences, however, I was much ahead of the average and not far behind the best. And their advantage grew from the fact that their fathers and mothers knew how to read and write while mine did not.

To tell the truth, I learned more from listening to some of my elders than from my irregular attendance at school. There was old gray haired Melengo, the beggar, for instance. He was extremely ragged and dirty, but his mind was crystal-clear. He was always saying strange things that people would laugh at, as I did at that time. But now as I remember a few of his sayings they take on a profound significance. For instance, one of his favorite expressions was, "Humanity is a cyclone that does not come to moisten our fields, but, to flood them." Another was, "Sleep is a soft dagger that kills our day dreams – while we are young." And another, "Youth of woman is a boiling cauldron and love the over-brimming water that quenches its flames."

Melengo had been to South America in his youth and had led a wild life the very mention of which made the women of our town turn their eyes in horror toward heaven.

There was also Alberto, the shepherd, a tall man with square bronzed face and an immense hairy chest. He was one of the best known shepherds of that region and enjoyed a popular renown as the only shepherd who would tell the truth. His attitude of thoughtful resignation was sublime. Whatever might happen, he merely regarded it as part of his daily chore. The spirits walked with him in the twilight splendor of the upper mountains and the aerial invisible powers had full control of his mind. If there was trouble or sorrow "it was the will of those whose methods are not for us to understand."

Alberto was a remarkable player of the bagpipe – that poetic, eternal instrument of the solitary shepherds. And I remember how on an autumn evening he would sit on a bench not far from our door. And while the great sun vanished into an abyss of red, he would play rich harmonious music that was born, even as he was, out of those mystic mountains.

One winter Alberto went down with his sheep toward the green plains of Apulia and failed to return with the spring. I never could find out exactly what caused his death. Perhaps he vanished one night and followed his invisible companions into the haunted solitudes. Who knows?

By the time I was twelve I stopped going to school entirely and began my life of continuous toil. It is, in fact, the custom among us for boys and girls, on reaching twelve to stop attending school to become either a household instrument or a little farmer.

Everybody works. There is poverty. Often there is not enough to eat. There are among us many women whose husbands have gone to alien lands. Sometimes money does not come from across the sea. Perhaps the father is out of work, perhaps he has been hurt in an accident or even killed. These women do not waste much time in crying. They take up the task of keeping the household going with as little expense as possible. Everyone in their family must help, down to the children barely able to walk.

Everyone works. The mother will probably hire

a small piece of land and cultivate it. If she has a baby it is placed under the shade of the nearest tree. And the strong mother tills and finally harvests the products of their collective toil.

Perhaps a drought comes. Then the streams dry up. Frantically, the mother will work over the shrunken and yellow plants. And probably, after a long struggle she will have to abandon her field, in despair, and leave the sickly plants to die under the merciless sun.

Droughts are the terror of our valley and often have I seen people with hunger in their eyes gazing upward at the serene blue sky and begging for rain.

Both my parents worked out in the fields and received a small pittance for wages. And I too had to help them intermittently from the time I was very young. And I can safely say that work rather than school was the important element in my boyhood. We were very poor people. We rarely had meat, and our food was of the poorest kind. Yet we were happy. There was no such thing as sickness among us. In fact, the inhabitants of our valley are among the tallest and most finely developed people in all Italy. And many of our women who work out on the fields at the side of their husbands are stronger than the men.

I was at twelve a large nimble boy. I would have liked to play. And while toiling in the hot sun blaze of the fields I would dream of the cool upper reaches of the mountains. And of the plump yellow lizards that we boys hunted by the hedgerows. And the games and escapades dear to the hearts of boys. But when the excessive work of spring and harvest time was over, then I would pasture my sheep up on the mountains that I loved. And I had no cares, and I would sing to myself, pausing perhaps to hear my own echo descending upon me.

The inspiration of Monte Majella above me, I later sought to express in a poem, which after many vicissitudes was finally printed in *The Nation*:

The mountain in a prayer of questioning heights
    gazes upward at the dumb heavens,
And its inner anger is forever bursting forth
In twisting torrents.
Like little drops of dew trickling along the crevices
Of this giant questioner
I and my goats were returning toward the town
    below.
But my thoughts were of a little glen where wild
    roses grow
And cool springs bubble up into blue pools.
And the mountain was insisting for an answer from
    the still heaven.

CHAPTER III

There is a continuous stream of beggars from strange places that passes through our town. Especially during festive days when they crowd the entrances of Introdacqua. And it seems that many of them find it so pleasant and the people so generous that they make a sort of permanent abode in our midst. Yet the givers themselves are very poor, though rich in kindness. What alms they hand out consist mostly of pieces of bread, a cutting of salted pork or a plate of soup. And usually they add a glass or two of the best wine in the house, with sincere impartiality.

This vast tribe of human derelicts is mostly composed of cripples, lame creatures hardly able to struggle along, and those struck by disease or by absolute poverty. Into this sad torrent there has intrusively entered a more evil element, namely, those who play on the superstitions and fear of the simple country people. So we find witches, vampires and wizards demanding food and respect from the poor peasants and getting it.

Like a dark promontory of fright overshadowing a craving sea of beggars, loomed a strange woman in our town. She had come from the weird barrens of the mountains, before I was born, and had made her home among us. She was gazed at, but scarcely seemed to see anyone as she passed through the crooked streets of our town. Yet a shudder ran through the hearts of all who beheld her, especially those mothers with small children.

Whenever this woman loomed darkly in the sunny doorway of a house, there was an instinctive handing forth of gifts, with trembling hands. And the peasant wife would fall white-faced into a chair when the shadow had passed.

When I was about six I first began to notice this weird creature. She was old and ugly then. Yet people whispered that in her youth she had been of strange loveliness, when she haunted the upper mountains and the blue spaces of Majella. And it was said that the sneers of a young shepherd had brought her down to haunt our town. She was the daughter of a terrible wizard who lived on the mother mountain. And now this lovely creature had become old and shrunken; but her eyes had a strange majesty in them.

Whenever she would try to enter our house I and my brothers would hide ourselves under our parents' bed, trembling with fear. For this woman was generally reputed to be a vampire; and to anger her was almost certain death.

When I got to be about nine I was told in all seriousness by an adult that if anyone put salt on her head and then observed her actions, it could be plainly seen that she was a vampire. For as soon as salt touched her hair she would scream and writhe in agony. And a plain woman would not have been so strangely affected by it. All of this awoke the curiosity in us boys to put salt on the old hag's head. And there were many attempts and ambushes, but she seemed to be fortunate in eluding our best laid plans. And besides, we always felt very tremulous at her approach, especially if we held some accusing salt.

Time passed. Some of the older lads, when in a group, would attempt to give this woman some slight annoyance. To put salt on her head was a sort of golden goal for most of us boys. But we always had to run for it; for whenever she saw us coming and thought we meant mischief, she would bend, pick up a stone and heave it violently after us, shouting strange words that made our hearts quake.

I remember one day, though, when this wild creature allowed us to approach her. It was a beautiful September afternoon when the rosy cheeks of the mature apples beautify their laden branches; when the various fields of grape are quickly ripening and the figs lure the passerby with their boughs spread to the broad sun.

She was squatted on the soft grass in the cool shadow and began to murmur to herself. She was mumbling something about *stregoneria*, or witchcraft. Gradually, one by one, a group of women and children gathered around her, listening to her weird words. Within their minds, long ploughed and harrowed by superstition, the mutterings of the hag took root quickly. They all gazed as if fascinated. I remember I was peering from between two fat women while she spoke of her powers.

Finally the hag stopped, ending a sentence in air, and with eyes half-shut, arose. And she began the round of the village asking alms as usual. The startled group followed at a respectful distance.

Whatever was given her, whether potatoes, corn, pieces of bread or salt pork, she put together into a large sack. When it was full she tightened the end of it, slung it on her head, and started toward her home on the edge of the town. And her eyes were gleaming and always glancing around, watchful for boys and girls who would try to put salt on her head – to discover her dark secrets.

This was her life. When the food was consumed, she would reappear – to the terror of the town. She was also very clever, and knew how to vary her rounds so as not to visit one place too often. She also kept clear of the isolated places in the country where they kept bad dogs who would attack her, witch or no witch.

There were a few of the bolder men, also, who refused to give her anything, but their wives usually made up the difference with the witch in secret.

Now it happened, when I was about thirteen, that there was a big holiday in our town in honor of its patron saints. A large group of men were gathered in the tavern. And as is usual with men, after a few applications of wine, they seemed to have reached the acme of eloquence. Each had a good deal to say about some favorite subject that came within their knowledge. And the hours passed with plenty of wine and topics consumed.

While they were joking at each other, one of the men's wives happened to go there and beg her husband to go home.

One of the more drunken men shouted at her, "Don't be afraid, don't be afraid, there are no women here to rob your husband!"

There was another man in the place and he was leaning against the wall, apparently asleep. But the drunken fellow, turning, noticed him and shouted jovially to wake him up.

Now when a man falls asleep in a conversation, we have two or three choice expressions for it. We say, "Where has he been – irrigating his field last night?" or "Has he been stealing cucumbers?" or, finally, "What's the matter, has he been vampiring last night that he had no time to sleep?" It was the last expression that the drunkard used.

Immediately the conversation started upon the subject of vampires. It was an amusing lot of superstition, I remember, for I was there with my father. Some horrible anecdotes were told, in all seriousness. And I can say that, what with the wine and the gruesome subject, they were all impressed. Time passed, and still the conversation went on, with increasing zest.

The other wives came. Some brought their children along; and they all began to shout that it was time to go home – as it really was. All of them were invited to drink by their husbands or brothers. Some of the women laughed, one or two groaned and looked on statue-like, waiting for the breaking of the conversation. At the same time one of the most eloquent women among them – they were all eloquent on occasion – was directing her speech toward those who formed the stronghold of the conversation.

"Ah-ha!" exclaimed the woman, a portly being, "now is the time to go vampiring."

Another woman answered, "Oh yes! if you were that witch of Majella."

Just then one of the men staggered to his feet, and turning slowly, imperious with wine, shouted to his wife, "Don't give her anything more – not a crumb! Do you understand? Or else I'll settle with you!" And growling curses about the hag he brought his fist down on the table.

He was a tall handsome young man, with dark eyes and curly black hair and a complexion more dusky than most of us. His wife, a little blue-eyed woman was accustomed to obey him. They had only been married about two years, and had one child, a pretty boy.

And with a general round of drunken curses against the witch the conversation broke up. But as we turned to go out, someone whispered, "There she is!"

A low moon hovered over the ragged edge of the mountains. The street in front of the tavern was flooded with a ghostly light. And darkly through this pallor receded slowly the black looming form of the witch.

"She was here!"

"She has been listening to us!"

Many hurried conjectures were made. I dare say most of the men and women were frightened and, to atone, gave the witch extra portions of tribute when she called again at their homes.

But the wife of that tall peasant did not. Somehow the husband's command clung to her memory.

One day the witch stood in dark silent threat on the threshold.

Quickly the wife blurted out the words that she had been repeating to herself several days, "Go! I cannot give you anything – go!"

The hag opened her dreamy eyes wide and glistening. "Ah! You have changed!" she exclaimed, "and so suddenly, eh?"

Just then the husband approached with a *bidento* on his shoulders. Quickly running up and cursing wildly he drove the old hag away. She hurried on, muttering evilly. From within the house came the cries of a baby.

After that their son, a beautiful boy of six months, began to sicken. Alarmed, the mother went to see the doctor, probably an incompetent one. He gave the child some medicine which didn't do any good.

In our valley a baby who cannot be relieved from an immediate illness will be at once classified as an innocent victim of the vampires.

The distracted mother went around getting advice from other women. They all knew what had happened. They came to the house, old and young.

Pathetically the mother sobbed, "My child! My child!"

Meanwhile the townswomen were examining the baby for any evidence of witchcraft. "Poor child!" they exclaimed discordantly, looking up, "it is reduced to bones – look! All skin and bones. And it was such a chubby little thing. The witch! The witch has taken hold of his life!"

One gaunt old woman exclaimed sharply, "She is too powerful. It's a pity – but I doubt whether the baby can be saved especially if she has passed the poor creature over the flames!"

And with heads bowed the women of the town went out leaving the sobbing mother.

I was lingering outside the door, in a shivering sort of curiosity. From what I gathered the witch must have entered as a spirit through the keyhole, for there were no horns in back of the door to prevent her. And putting the parents in a profound dream, she had taken the child. Outside she had invoked the spirit on which she rides through the storms.

In a second she had found herself beneath the great walnut tree of Benevento under which are spurting up mystic flames. There were many hags around all holding helpless infants. After they had drawn blood from them, the hags passed the little naked bodies over the flames. After that the children irreparably died – since no medicine in the world could save them. And the townswomen went on murmuring and tremulous.

Often the vampires themselves are fearful of their nocturnal prowlings and would escape the enchantment which binds them, if possible. But they are caught in the coils of some hideous diabolic power.

I was told of one unwilling vampire who asked a friend, a young housewife, to save her from the enchantment. The head wizard of the district was angered, but if the friend was courageous enough he could do nothing against them. If she was afraid they both would die.

So the vampire got on a horse with her friend and invoked the spirit of the storm, "I shall be the twenty-fourth in the procession that passes around the tree," she told the young lady, "do not forget!"

Immediately they were under the black gigantic tree whose heavy branches twisted and coiled across the starry sky.

The vampire jumped from the horse and rushed into the procession taking her place. The friend crouched to the ground outside the circle of light. When the procession approached, the unwilling vampire looked pleadingly toward her.

Immediately invoking the saints and the power of Ovidio, the young girl sprang at the hideous procession and pierced the woman with a needle. At the same instant they both vanished from that strange tribe, and each found herself in her own house. And the vampire, freed of all enchantment, became a most respectful and holy lady. And they both went to heaven at death, added my informer with grave nods.

This tale awoke in me the ambitious desire to pierce the old hag with a big needle. But – how to get near her was a problem. She had an especially evil eye for me because I was one of the most persistent of the salt throwers. I confided my ambition to my best friend, Antonio, and he immediately ran away from fright. But after a few hours he came back and announced that he was willing to aid me in my attempt.

The old witch was now more feared and respected than ever before. Some women brought her presents and begged her to free the baby of the enchantment. She grabbed the gifts with her bony hands and grinned upward, showing her yellow teeth. In horror they hurried away.

Meanwhile the poor mother who was waiting a short distance away sobbed over the child, "O unfortunate babe! The ugly witch wants you to die! I hide you on my breast, but the heavy sleep of the vampire wins me!"

And pressing the thin child to her breast she walked – almost staggered – home to prepare supper for her husband. He was coming back from wheat reaping where in place of his wife he had to hire another woman so that his wife could freely attend the sick child.

Unable to get near enough to the witch I and Antonio decided to try our needle on someone else. There was a poor fat old woman who puffed exceedingly whenever she moved her ponderous body through the town. I now believe that she was suffer-

ing from asthma. After much deliberation we two
decided that she was a vampire or about to become
one.

One evening, after dusk, we stole up behind her
and with a vigorous shove thrust a long needle into
her leg, piercing a few layers of petticoats.

With a shriek she turned about and instead of
thanking us proceeded to pummel and kick us until
we regained our wits and used our speedy legs.

This fiasco chilled our ardor for only a day or so.
And one night, not long afterwards, I remember, we
got our chance to pierce the witch! The village was
a dense twisting sea of gloom. The last light still
glimmered on the heights around the white town.
The castle, an indistinct giant form, stood lording
the black hollows. The pacing donkeys were returning with their owners riding on them through the
unlit darkness.

I and Antonio were prowling tremulously
through the town. Someone had told us that the
witch was about, having foraged for food all day.
We were scared, and pressed together from fright as
we walked. I had a formidable needle – as big as
what they used for sewing mattresses.

"Perhaps she will be cured," I whispered.

"And she may give us the gold she has hidden,"
he agreed.

Just as we turned a corner Antonio whispered,
"Sssh!"

The old hag was climbing a steep stony street to
one side. It was very dark there. Stealing up on tip-

toes, close to the line of houses we gradually approached her. She was going up very slowly, puffing and mumbling to herself. We were now a few feet away from her. Carefully, barefooted, we made no sound and were undiscovered. We paused. Antonio was pushing my arm as if to say, "You do it." I was pushing his arm. She kept going up. Now was our chance. All at once a determination possessed me and I sprang out toward her. I was just two steps from her, needle raised in my hand, when she wheeled about with a fearsome yell and raised her bony arms.

I saw her looming above me, her fingers twisted, her eyes wide open and her sharp teeth gleaming. With a cry of pain and fear I and Antonio rushed headlong down the street. And we didn't stop running until we had reached our homes.

For a few days I and my friend kept as close to our houses as possible. To tell the truth I hardly slept for almost a week expecting always to see the hideous vampire hovering over me at night.

About a month had passed since the child was first seized by the mysterious consuming malady, and report had it that the little tot could not live more than another week.

A big black cat – probably astray – had been seen prowling near the baby's cradle. Everyone swore that it was the witch, which was conclusive evidence. The mother herself was getting sick from sorrow and worry.

The young father was frantic and walked fiercely through the streets. "If she has anything to revenge, or any spite to do, why does she make our little innocent son the victim?" he would say. "Why doesn't she revenge herself upon me? But I'll make her pay for this." And with a peasant's insistence, as if hypnotized by the words, he kept repeating, "Why must an innocent baby suffer for its parents' folly? Why must the innocent suffer?"

One morning there was a great talk and uproar in Introdacqua. It was reported that the witch had been driven from the town. The father had gathered some of his braver relatives and *compari* and they had beaten and driven the hag out into the night and destroyed the hut in which she lived.

Immediately we all rushed up to see the ruins of her home. There was a great crowd on the hilly ground, all keeping at a respectful distance from the pile of stones and cinders.

Many of the women were visibly alarmed and were crying to one another that the witch's father – the eternal wizard of Majella – would in vengeance destroy our town.

But the autumn days passed and nothing happened. A great shadow seemed to be lifted from our town. The witch had disappeared up in the mountains and no one knew where she was.

One day I was pasturing my goats and sheep on the broad shoulder of the immense mountain. Higher and higher we went, gradually leaving the castle below us, and reaching the clear bright regions of stunted trees and fitful mountain storms. Far below me was the white town and to the north stretched

the vast glorious valley that was for so many centu-
ries the stronghold of the mighty Samnites. In a hazy
softness of distance it appeared, threaded by the
Pescara, the blue river. There gleamed Sulmona, sur-
rounded by its towered walls. And there nestled the
villages of the Marsi, and further north, though hidden in mists, I knew was Aquila, the city of the eagle.

A continuous movement stirred the pure air. The
animals were ever cropping grass before me as I pas-
tured them higher and higher toward the rocky flanks
of the upper peaks.

There was something dark like a black boulder at
the end of a long grassy stretch in front of me. In
curiosity, on my guard, I approached it, gripping
my strong cudgel.

Just as I was about five steps away, it sprang up
throwing out arms enclosed in black rags. With a
gasp of horror I stopped short. There in front of me,
tall and erect, stood the fearsome witch.

I had the impulse to turn and scamper down the
mountain, abandoning all, sheep, goats, staff.

But as I looked up at her, in fright, I felt a strange
feeling of pity. There was no hatred, no anger in her
gray eyes. There was an animal fear. I have seen it in
the eyes of young helpless birds. Her arms were very
thin and bony, one of her feet had been wounded,
probably on the sharp stones of the mountains, and
she had tied a woolen rag around it.

For a moment we looked at one another there,
high up on the solitary mountains. She did not appear to see me, for her eyes seemed to gaze through

me as through a crystal to some point far beyond, beyond the skies. Then her mouth opened, and in a piteous weak voice she cried, "I am hungry!"

Without hesitating, as if obeying a command, I took my scanty lunch from the bag slung over my shoulder and handed it to her. Quickly she stepped forward and grabbed it. And ravenously, cramming her mouth and staring around with wild eyes, she consumed the food. As if fascinated, fearing and pitying her, I watched the poor creature gulping down my food. When she had finished she looked around as if for more. I took a step backward, still nervously gripping my staff.

At that moment her eyes gazed into mine. Her face brightened. And for the first time in my life I saw her smile.

"Boy! Boy!" she sobbed softly. "Thank you!" and she opened her bony arms as though to embrace me.

With awakened horror and fear I shrank back. She stopped, her arms still outstretched. The smile vanished from her face. And of a sudden she must have realized how hideous and repulsive she was – and of a sudden she must have realized what a twisted horror her life had been.

As if felled by an invisible blow, she dropped on her face among the stones. And sobbing, fitfully, terribly like a mother who had lost her child, she rolled from side to side. What thoughts must have filled her – what remorse – what horror at herself!

I stepped back, hesitating. She still sobbed, rolling her emaciated body from side to side on the stony ground. Then, panic stricken, I turned. I beat my goats and sheep and they fled noisily down the mountainside. I ran after them seized with sudden fear. And I left the old hag up there on the bright mountain, sobbing in the calm golden sunlight.

Down I went, down, into the village, trembling with an ever-growing fear. My mother wanted to know why I had returned so early. I told them. The women neighbors who had gathered around gasped. And for more than a week I was under close observation by the women to see if I showed any symptoms of illness or witchcraft.

Now the autumn days began to dwindle and the pressure of duty lessened quickly for most of the year's work had been accomplished. One day, the baby, after a long illness of pain, died.

The father said little except what had become a habit with him, "Why did she make the innocent suffer?"

Storms whirled through our valley. The upper mountains now glittered with frost in the early mornings. One day when looking out from my house I saw the rocky region where I had met the hag, a soft glistening white. Report had it that the inclement weather was slowly driving her downward toward the town.

Meanwhile the father was swearing vengeance and wandering aimlessly around the town and on the highlands.

One morning the witch was found badly beaten near a stream that passes through our town. She was in a very bad condition. She had a bag alongside her in which were found a few almost uneatable roots and other wild things. The flesh had been almost worn from her bony fingers, probably through digging for roots.

She was still conscious when they found her. The chief of police asked her who had beaten her. She shook her head and they say that tears appeared in her dull eyes.

The next night, while a glorious moon was flaring above the snowy heights, the reports slowly circulated that the vampire was dead.

It was a strange night, weird, intriguing. It was perhaps such a night as I later attempted to describe in a poem called "Fantasio" which afterwards appeared in *The Measure*.

FANTASIO

As Night like a black flower shuts the sun within its
    petals of gloom,
The silent road crosses the sleeping valley like a
    winding dream –
While the whole region has succumbed under the
    weight of a primeval silence.
The mountains like mighty giants lift themselves
    with a regal haughtiness out of the ruling gloom.
Across the dim jagged distances are pearl-gray wings
    flitting
Flitting –

The moonlight is a hailstorm of splendor

Pattering on the velvet floor of gloom –
The moon!
The moon is a faint, memory of a lost sun –
The moon is a footprint that the Sun has left on
     pathless heaven!
Pearl-gray wings are whirling distantly –
Whirling!
A fever of youth streams through my being
Trembling under the incantation of Beauty,
Like a turmoil of purple butterfly caught in a web
     of light.

A black foam of darkness overflows from the rim of
     night,
And floods away the pearl-gray wings!

CHAPTER IV

One evening, when I was fifteen, I found my mother crying softly but bitterly. As soon as I entered our hut she wiped her eyes and tried to assume a calm expression. To my repeated questions she shook her head. I asked where my father was. She pointed out toward the fields.

It was swiftly getting dark. A few dim lights began to show here and there in the village. And on the road before our house the richer peasants were returning on their slow donkeys through the vast gloom. My father had none, for we were far too poor to own any.

Again I looked at my mother. She was leaning her arm on the narrow window sill with her chin between her fingers. Under her raven black hair, her face appeared pale in the dim glow of twilight. Almost everybody we knew had already passed on their way home. The bells rang distantly.

I was alarmed, especially at her ominous silence for I knew that my mother was not a woman to show much visible signs of emotion. No woman who works harder than most men out in the fields tilling the soil can do that. I had been helping a neighbor at harvest for two cents a day. She was here alone without either my father or my younger brother.

Finally, I begged her almost in a sobbing voice to tell me what had happened.

She turned. "Nothing," she said, "I am just thinking."

"But where are they?"

"There was a large spot of wheat that is too ripe and your father is trying to mow it all. Otherwise the strong winds that are blowing tonight may shake it to the ground. I came home to make supper. Do you want to eat now, or will you wait for them?"

I was famished, but I decided to wait. The minutes passed very slowly. A thick moonless gloom had now completely enveloped our valley. Fitful whirls of wind were softly whistling here and there. Finally we heard footsteps. And after a few seconds, the door was flung open and my brother came running in followed by my tall father.

I noticed that both he and my mother stared at each other coldly, almost as if enemies. I was wondering what could have come between them.

My brother happened to go upstairs and I went up the steep ladder after him. In a low voice I asked him if he knew what was the matter. He shook his head and said that he had not noticed anything wrong save one small incident. That afternoon, while working in the merciless sun, all at once, in a fit of disgust, my father had thrown down his tools and had trudged to the other end of the field. My mother had walked after him and they had talked together for a long while in a low voice. After that my mother had come home.

As we came down, I heard my father say in an earnest voice, "I cannot help it. Otherwise we will never get out of this quicksand."

They stopped talking as soon as they saw us. And we sat down to a silent meal of hot chicory and rice soup. Sleep soon overwhelms the tired peasant, and after a moody silence my father went up to bed. My brother followed. My mother and I remained behind. I stood for a few minutes looking at her.

Then I begged her to please tell me what it was that oppressed her.

She sighed deeply and whispered, "Your father has decided to go away."

Alarmed I exclaimed, "Where to?"

"To America."

I felt a wild pain, for I dearly love my father. To America! I had heard much of that strange place into which people we knew had vanished and had never returned. Had never returned! And my own father! After all, I was a young boy, and I could not keep back the tears.

My mother put her arms around me and pressed her toil-marked face in my hair. And she kissed me, begging me not to cry. I looked up into her beautiful eyes and I was calmed.

Sighing deeply, she murmured, "I cannot blame him. He works so hard. And we never seem to get any better. I must bend myself to what has to be."

Still I sobbed at the thought that my father would go away. But she, with a mother's divine art, softly calmed me. And smiling into my eyes, she begged me to go to gentle dreams. So, slowly, together we went up the ladder into our unlit bedroom.

Our people have to emigrate. It is a matter of too much boundless life and too little space. We feel tied up there. Every bit of cultivable soil is owned by those fortunate few who lord over us. Before spring comes into our valley all the obtainable land is rented out or given to the peasants for a season under usurious conditions, namely, for three-fourths, one-half or one-fourth of the crops, the conditions depending upon the necessity either of the owner or of the peasant who is seeking land. Up to a few years ago some peasants had to take land even on the one-fifth basis; that is, the man who worked the land and bought even seeds and manure would only get one-fifth of the harvest, while the owner who merely allowed him to use the land would receive four-fifths. This was possible up to a short while ago. But today such a thing is absolutely impossible since no peasant would agree to it unless his head were not functioning normally. And what is it that saves the man and keeps him from being ground under the hard power of necessity? The New World!

Previously, there was no escape; but now there is. In the old days men from our highlands did go down into the marshes of Latium to harvest and earn some extra money. And there they sickened with malaria and came back ghosts of their former selves. But now there was escape from the rich landowners, from the terrors of drought, from the spectre of starvation, in the boundless Americas out of which at times people returned with fabulous tales and thousands of liras – riches unheard of before among peasants.

The year before, my father had been trying to better our conditions. He had hired two large pieces of arable ground on which he had toiled almost every minute of daylight during that whole season. Having no money to make the first payment on the land, he had to borrow some at a very high rate of interest. At the end of that season, after selling the crops, he found that he had just barely enough money to pay the rest of the rent and to pay back the loan with the enormous interest. It is the landowners and the moneylenders who are the real vampires among us – not pitiable, demented old women.

That season of excessive toil made my father much older. His tall strong body was beginning to bend. He had become a little clumsy and slower. And the results of his futile attempt made him moody and silent. He would sit on our door-step in the evenings and gaze out at the living darkness of our valley. At times, when one talked to him he would answer very absently as if his thoughts were far away.

And finally, the inevitable decision came into his mind and he was not to be moved from it.

The next morning I noticed several times that my mother was gazing anxiously after me as I set about getting ready for my day's work. She seemed gentler than usual as if she were trying, as much as she could, to make me happy and satisfied. I went to my work where I did not have time to do any thinking.

When I returned I noticed that she scanned my face with a timid anxiety. Once I called her to ask her a question and she stopped short and turned white.

And so it was that day after day my mother strove piteously, frantically to make me contented and satisfied. She knew how much I loved my father, and her mother's fears foretold what actually came to pass even before I thought about it.

At first I felt boyishly angry against this America which was stealing my father from me. Then I became boyishly curious. In the evenings my mother had been smiling so much and had made many wonderful promises of the new happy life we would lead when my father returned from America laden with riches. I began to think that this new land was quite a desirable place. She would tell me how we would have a house which I always desired, and two pigs, and how our neighbors would all respect us, and the *signori* in the town would even deign to talk to us sometimes. The result of all this was to make me more and more curious about a land which could confer such blessings.

With everything in her power my poor mother tried to keep the idea of going away from my mind. But it was inevitable. One day, I hardly know how, I began to think that I would go with my father. Surely I could earn as much as he in the new land, for I was as big and as strong as any fully developed man. And our blessing would be double if I went, or else we would return in half the time and all be together again.

My mother noticed the change in me. She knew my decision as soon as I came in, for her eyes became alarmed. I felt a wild pity and sorrow, for young as I was I realized how she must have felt at seeing her little family break away from her.

As we sat down for supper my father remarked to her, "What has happened – are you sick?"

She shook her head and bravely tried to smile. Her timid kindness to me at the table that night almost killed me. I could hardly contain myself any more. But fortunately our poor, scanty supper did not last long.

Slowly my father trudged up the ladder. I heard his heavy, tired footsteps as he walked around getting ready to go to sleep. It was a soft mellow night. Dazed with conflicting thoughts I walked out to the steps and sat down wearily. Without a word, my mother came and sat at my side. We did not look at each other. For a long while we sat there staring at the purple valley before us.

Softly, hesitating, my mother whispered my name. I turned my face to her. Her eyes were gazing at me in sorrow and love. Her lips moved tremulously. But not a sound came forth from them. I realized that I had never been away from her love even one night.

As we gazed at one another her voice came in a soft despair, "You too – want to go away."

I did not answer. I bowed my head lower and lower.

Sobbing, she threw her arms about me and pressed me to her breast. In the darkness of her tight embrace, eyes closed, I wept. We both wept there on the steps. She kissed my lips again and again. Her warm tears fell on my face. I was sobbing, "I will return soon, we will return soon." But no. Her mother's fears foretold the truth. I never returned. Again she embraced me, as she did when she would cradle me to sleep on her breast. Again she kissed me. And so we remained for a long, long while until a tranquil peace came upon us.

"Children are like birds after big strong wings have grown and enabled them to fly, very seldom they think of returning back home to the mother's bough. I know! I know!"

CHAPTER V

Quickly we set about making plans for leaving. My father had wished to take me along even before my decision, but hated to separate me from my mother, though he thought of me all the time. Nor did he oppose my desire to accompany him.

My mother, soon resigned, began to make us various pairs of socks, both of cotton and of wool shorn from our neighbor's lambs. Another man in the hamlet had also decided to go. He had been married for about two years and had great ambitions and little money. As the first move he went to town and bought himself a substantial valise.

His wife was a very beautiful woman with a temper rather stronger than the average. With multitudinous tears she steadily refused to do anything for her husband, hoping to hold him back by her unpreparedness. But he had decided and tears and spite were of no avail. Realizing this she began later on, with a quicker pace, to prepare all the articles he might need.

We heard of many others in the town who were leaving. Some of them had rich *compari* and relatives. Dinners were being given in their honor before their departure. As for us, we were growing more and more eager each day. There was still work for us; we toiled up to the last day of our departure, just as we resumed work the second day after our arrival in America.

With a few others in our town, my father arranged to go to work in America for a foreman on the state roads who was a fellow-townsman.

Many times the wives would get together mournfully and talk of the parting. Doubt gnawed at their hearts, for instances were well known of husbands who had gone away and had never returned, or whose letters had suddenly stopped. Accidents, perhaps death, perhaps a new-grown indifference were the not infrequent causes of such breaks.

All that winter my mother toiled incessantly to mend our clothes and weave new things for us. But we were very poor and she found it hard to get any material. Nevertheless she worked on and did the best she could.

The parting day came. It was Wednesday. All our relatives made it a holiday and we had a substantial dinner – a dinner as good as when my parents got married, they all agreed. We were dressed in our finest and our little hut was well cleaned. The neighbors had all come around to scan us curiously, as though they had not seen us for so many years. We all smiled, my mother most of all. And then the parting.

We walked slowly toward the station. One of our relatives tried to make a witty remark. We felt lighthearted. Then, of a sudden, an overwhelming sense of horror and pain possessed me as I thought that I was leaving my mother.

"God bless you," she was saying, trying her best to smile through the tears that trickled down her cheeks.

I sobbed.

The others who were sailing on the same ship left at the same time, and the scene at the station was one of undescribable confusion, lamentation and exclamation.

Up rumbled the train which traveled without any horses or mules. I felt my father urging me aboard. A last kiss from my mother. Everything was obscured by a mist of tears. We were going into the unknown. Had our feet been carrying us we would have instinctively turned toward home.

But the train sped along.

It was the first time in my life I had been on a train, and it was a remarkable experience. The first tunnel we rumbled into, with its sudden blotting of all light, nearly frightened me to death and made me stop sobbing. Out we flashed. The whole world seemed moving around. Hills and mountains were moulding and curving toward us, their white villages growing and then gradually fading off into their green indistinct folds.

Finally I saw a thrilling sight. We had just come out of a tunnel and were speeding at a high, rare altitude toward the plains of Campania. Sparkling and flashing in the distance and spreading right across the world was something all in motion. At first I was frightened. Then I thought, "The sea! That must be what they call the sea!"

And it was. We sped into Naples.

Here it was a continuous startling whirl. Every-thing had been arranged for us in advance by the agent for the steamship company. We were taken to a lodging house to await the ship's departure.

On first reaching the place we were subjected to a physical examination. They made sure that our teeth and eyes were in proper shape, but were not so eager about our purses. Three times these examina-tions were repeated, until the fourth day after our arrival in Naples when the steamship "Cedric" left port.

The hour approached. With all our baggage we stood on line awaiting our turn to go aboard. It was with a quailing heart and a sense of great misgiving that I stepped on the immense steel vessel. For I en-tertained great doubts as to whether the whole af-fair could stay afloat for many days. It being rather late when we got on board, we ate a little and went down to our sleeping quarters.

That night we slept below in our iron berths. A man nearby remarked, "We must be already past Sardinia."

"Good heavens! How far!" exclaimed another.

I thought, "Good heavens! How far – that we have so easily passed Sardinia – whatever it may be!"

I remember as in a dream the flashing seas around Gibraltar and the vendors of oranges who came alongside the ship in their little boats.

The voyage was a nightmare, interposed with mo-ments of strange brilliance. We passed the Azores which looked like toy islands with toy houses and windmills. No sooner had they vanished under the horizon than a tremendous storm rolled into us. We were locked under deck and our fate was placed in the hands of others.

I must confess that I was terrified, as were most of my fellow-travelers in the steerage. We felt our own helplessness. The ship swayed incessantly. At dinner plates of undesired soup would rise or slide in a most spiteful manner, perhaps ending their peregrinations on our laps. To tell the truth we were not much oppressed by hunger during that terrible storm. Outside, the end of the world might have come for all that we could conceive of the tremendous wrath of the elements as the angry waters poured across the portholes.

One man in a wild anxiety, perhaps anxious to see if there was any way of escape, unbolted a porthole and looked out. Immediately a shining flood of water poured in. Two sailors came running up cursing angrily. The man blinked and remonstrated with them. They shouted. He pulled out a knife. Others came to pull them apart. And the noisy waves outside added to the hullabaloo.

During a comparative calm we were allowed to stagger out on deck. Then came one of our innocent sports: namely, looking at the fishes.

Some would cry, "See the fishes!"

"Where? Where?" And we would all rush to the side to stare down in amusement at the playful antics of shining porpoises that swam alongside the vessel. They would follow us for immense distances and for many hours we would forget our terrors of the vast ocean in gazing down at the beautiful creatures.

It was a foggy day when we finally approached New York Harbor, too late to enter. For hours out we had seen small boats with white sails, and finally we beheld a twilight strip of shore which gradually vanished under a curtain of mist and darkness. Still it was land – it was America! The terrors which the boundless mid-ocean had waked in us soon vanished and left us in easeful relief. We strolled happily along the deck. Some of those who had been here before were unsuccessful in trying to point out Coney Island to us.

Below all was confusion and noise. Everyone was talking at once. Gradually, however, a silence came over some of us. There was a hideous doubt in our minds. No one was sure either of entering America or being sent back as undesirable – which would mean a ruined life. For many of us had come on loaned money whose interest alone we would barely be able to pay when we got back.

We went to Ellis Island where we were inspected and examined. I really did not find any of the bad treatment and manhandling that some tender-skinned immigrants complain about. Anyhow, on the 20th of April, 1910, I and my father with a crowd of our fellow townsmen were allowed to land in America!

Mario Lancia, our new foreman, met us at the

Battery. He shook hands with all of us and remarked on my having grown into a broad, husky lad. I grinned and turned startled at the sight of an elevated train dashing around the curve towards South Ferry. To my surprise, not even one car fell. Nor did the people walking beneath scurry away at its approach as I would have done.

Chattering happily, we started to cross a broad street. All at once there was a terrific crash overhead, a car clanged before us, two automobiles whirled around. Another car was bearing down on our group.

"Here's the car," said the foreman and then, smiling, explained the roar to me. "It's only the train over us."

I felt as if those unseen wheels above were grinding paths through my own body. The car came up and stopped without knocking any one of us down as we stood awkwardly in its way with our multicolored bundles.

We climbed into a strange vision. The marvelous foreman spoke some words in an unknown language to a uniformed man who received money. And the uniformed person looked sneeringly at the wonderful foreman.

We sat down. A most inconceivable vision was flashing past the car window. As we traveled on, and my dazed eyes became accustomed to the place I began to look around. A matronly lady sitting opposite was scanning me with a sort of pitying gaze. I wondered whether I should get up and bow to her. Then I noticed that right next to the lady sat a father and son. Upright and straight, they were both glaring at a newspaper which the father held. With compassion, I observed that they were both afflicted with some nervous disease, for their mouths were in continuous motion, like cows chewing cud. "Too bad," I thought, "that both father and son should be afflicted in the same way!"

The foreman was anxious, pulling out a watch continually and saying that we had barely time to catch a train for our final destination. So we were not to live in this remarkable place! And now, just before we reached the station, I began to notice that there were signs at the corners of the streets with "Ave.! Ave.! Ave.!" How religious a place this must be that expresses its devotion at every crossing, I mused. Still, they did not put the "Ave." before the holy word, as, in "Ave Maria," but rather after. How topsy-turvy!

What confusion greeted us at the station! We hurried through a vast turning crowd and dashed down toward a train. Almost before realizing it, we were speeding toward our destination, Hillsdale, where work was ready for us on the state road. I was overwhelmed, but pleased.

CHAPTER VI

And this was America, I thought. During our way over on the ship I had seen golden heaps of clouds and rainbow vistas toward which we sped, and I had come to believe that they were perhaps the portals of America.

But this place was out in a forest, a soft murmuring woodland of enormous trees, straight and majestic. In our country large forests are a rarity. And trees were practically all planted by the hands of man. But these giant trees were monuments. And as the sunlight poured through them I felt small and helpless – almost lost.

We went down a coiling mud-road on a truck which had met us at the station. And after a long ride through the woods we came out upon a clearing in the center of which was a small, smoky wooden shack. That was to be our home. We jumped down. A man came to the door. I had heard of him. There several other men, all fellow-townsmen, who were waiting for our arrival to complete the new gang.

It was getting dark in the forest. A golden twilight poured over the trees. Some birds chirped in an ugly voice.

Inside the shack we were setting our things in

order. Someone played on a mandolin. My father at the threshold was admiring the tall straight trees. And finally, we sat down around a long table in the glow of a kerosene lamp while one of the men served us with delicious soup.

And there we all were, at the beginning of our long years of toil together in America. In this country immigrants of the same town stick together like a swarm of bees from the same hive, and work wherever the foreman or "boss" finds a job for the gang. And we who had been thrown together almost by chance became like one family, until a few years later when death and troubles finally separated us.

Our original gang was of the family type, all quiet, hard-working men. We had known one another more or less in Introdacqua. But by the time we were settled in Hillsdale we were like very close relatives.

There was Matteo Rossi, a man of reasonable and pleasant character who always tried to avoid trouble, though I have seen few men who could compare with him in strength. A lack of necessary eloquence made him a dumb and almost inactive member of the gang. In the evenings, he would sit in a corner and listen to our foolish jests. So we called him, "the ace of hearts," a card which in one of our provincial games does very little. I believe he thought of his one little son all the time.

Giovanni Ferraro was a hilarious bachelor, just about entering his thirties. He was always talking about having to get married, and would eagerly listen when the men with families recounted their experiences. Perhaps he was anxious to learn something. He was a handsome man, almost blond, and somewhat slender compared to the rest of the gang. I believe he is still single.

Giorgio Vanno was a short elderly man of forty-five. He was almost as broad as he was high, and his arms and hands were enormous. He had clever brown eyes and was the champion talker of the gang. Sometimes the rest of us would launch a verbal attack upon him, and he all alone, would defend himself and probably defeat the whole crowd of us with his clever repartee.

Giacomo Gallina was not a very ready-fisted man, but somehow it never took him long to get into trouble. I never saw him in action, because he didn't stay long with us, but I did see some forlorn fellows on whom he had used his fists. He would have become a Dempsey, no doubt, with a little training, for he was one of the most perfectly built men I have ever seen. The only one among us who could compare with him was Andrea Lenta, who was called the giant of Introdacqua.

Andrea, six feet and a few more inches in height, was a dusky faced man, slow but powerful in his movements. He had a broad, hairy chest and unusually strong muscles. He believed – whether in jest or not, I am uncertain – that the world should be governed by individual strength. There should be no recourse to weapons or to courts. Of course, such a system would have made him one of the leaders of humanity. He was also the best educated among us, for he had married the daughter of one of the small tradesmen in our town, and she had taught him many things. He was always talking about Conradino, who was taken in a battle near Popoli, in our valley – whoever he was.

There was also Antonio Lancia with a stentorian voice. And if by any luck he could train it, no wireless apparatus would be necessary for the people on this globe when he would sing. The foreman, Mario Lancia, who was related to him, was very quiet and invariably kind. He was about forty years of age, and had passed almost half of his life in America. He could read and write some English, and was the guiding spirit of the gang.

Besides my father and me, there was another younger lad, Filippo, who was Matteo's nephew. I knew him well, for his father owned a piece of land near my home. I remember how, when little boys, we used to play together with almonds and walnuts during the autumnal spare time when there was no school and no sheep or goats to take care of. His uncle, Matteo, had charge of the young fellow in this strange country, and was saving up for him what money he earned, at first.

That night we were restless and anxious. Our beds were worse than at home just a few boards nailed together. The shack did not smell quite right either. Yet it was by far cleaner than many other shanties, in which I lived later on in America.

Early the next morning as the first light was pouring through the trees, we arose almost in a body. Everyone was talking. The foreman was showing one of them something. And I made my first acquaintance with the pick and shovel.

After a hasty breakfast we went out. A truck was in front of the shack. Another came lumbering up in back of it. The foreman shouted to the driver. "Come on!" "Yes – this one – no that one!" Confusion and endless talk as we all piled into the trucks.

Birds were still singing around with none too melodious voices. The morning air among the trees was fresh and sweet. Finally we got out upon the state road where we were to work. Some more gangs were already there. A few trucks filled with men came from another direction. We jumped down. A whistle blew harshly.

And we set to digging and handling our picks and shovels. And I have been handling them ever since.

We were digging a way through a hillock. The trucks came up, and we quickly filled them. Ahead some men were blasting a large outcropping rock. Each truck was quickly filled; another one came up; the driver jumped down. Eagerly, overflowing with newborn enthusiasm in this new bright land, we worked. Several of us, with Andrea and Giacomo looming among them, were attacking the brown hillside.

A group of men came past shouting in a strange language. That was probably the American language, which I had heard on my arrival in New York. A fight started up. Two men were pummeling each other. There were shouts, and their foreman rushed toward them white-faced with anger.

That noon we were pretty well tired and lay in the grateful shadow of some tall trees whose roots our excavation was exposing. One of the men who had been in America a few years came around with a couple of enormous pea pods – that is, I thought they were pea pods. But he stripped off the skin and giving us each a small piece of the pulpy center urged us to eat it. It was sweet and we were well pleased. He told us that they were called bananas. The name was easy to pronounce.

As we were about to resume our work, the foreman came up and began to talk to my father. After a few minutes they called me over.

"I want you to be water boy for a few days," said the foreman gravely.

I looked at my father. He nodded, so I nodded too.

The foreman showed me what to do, which was to bring pails of water to the men who worked and drank like truck horses. Filippo was already water boy, but as the gang was large I had to help him out until they got another lad. I was not at all insulted, even though I was as big and as strong as most of the men there. In fact, I enjoyed my easier duties.

I was at first much fascinated by the way they dumped sand and gravel from the trucks. A truck would come creaking up, filled with a mound of brown gravel. Right over the spot where the gravel was to be put, the truck would stop. Then the driver would step on something which I afterwards found out was a spring. The bottom of the truck would open outward like a double door. The driver shouted to his horses and the truck lumbered away with its flapping bottom while the gravel was neatly deposited in a big mound. This seemed to me to be the very height of cleverness. Nor did I suspect at the time how soon I was to experience the full cleverness of the contrivance.

That night we were going home, piled in the trucks. Fresh was the breeze and calm the countryside. Slowly we entered into the great looming forest. We were all very fatigued from our long hours, ten of labor and one of lunch, making eleven in all. I was listening to the droning sounds of the crickets. A few of the men were joking; the others, their red faces shining with sweat, were leaning around in the truck. The second truck with four others and the foreman followed.

Something happened, and all of a sudden the bottom seemed to have fallen out of creation, and with an unpleasant thud we hit the hard ground, surprised and startled, while the truck slowly moved over us. For a moment we lay there between the wheels gaping as they passed off. Then we began to shout, yell and curse. Giacomo, who was one of those dumped so unceremoniously out of his restful reveries, jumped to his feet wild with anger. Cursing, he leaped toward the truck driver. My father and the foreman held him back. Another one who

fell also sought to soothe his wounded feelings by
wounding the driver. The poor fellow had jumped
down from his seat, and nervously gripping his whip,
was endeavoring to explain that it was an accident
– how springs sometimes came loose of themselves.
Well, since nothing worse than a few bruises had
come out of the accident, we were appeased, and
climbed in again, a little suspicious of the tricky, diabolic contraption. And so the first days passed.

None of us, including myself, ever thought of a
movement to broaden our knowledge of the English
language. We soon learned a few words about the
job, that was the preliminary creed; then came
"bread," "shirt," "gloves" (not kid gloves), "milk."
And that is all. We formed our own little world –
one of many in this country. And the other people
around us who spoke in strange languages might
have been phantoms for all the influence that they
had upon us or for all we cared about them.

Being water boy with the gang, I did the errands.
One of my first jobs in America was to go to the
village store about a mile away and buy a dozen
eggs. The foreman repeated the word, "aches," several times to me so that I could memorize it. And I
hurried down the road repeating the word to myself, so as not to forget it. But my debut in English
was somewhat unsuccessful, for by the time I got to
the grocery I had changed it to "axe," and with my
fingers I counted twelve.

Immediately the grocer, an old Polack, who didn't
understand much English himself, brought me a

dozen axes. I turned up my nose and shook my head. Then we began to use all the English we knew, which was quite negative as far as I was concerned. And finally, after a harmless and incomprehensible wrangling I made him understand that I was not a wood chopper; and that I hadn't come there with the slightest idea of buying his axes, even though he was insisting on showing me how fine they were, running his finger along the blade and nodding.

Then his wife came out into the dim store. She was fat, greasy and ugly, and understood less than her husband. Well, after they had shown me all sorts of objects, I began to illustrate my wish a little better and began to cackle like a hen. At first the wife appeared shocked. Then I made the sign of an oval with my fingers, at which they understood and brought out the eggs. And I went home in triumph.

Another little catastrophe happened during these early months when I was learning and misusing a few words of English. This occurred near Poughkeepsie, where we were not enjoying our first winter of American sleet and snow. It was January, the ground was thick with ice, and I was feeling angry. Filippo also felt angry. So we had a fight.

And after punching wildly, slipping and wrestling, we were both pretty well damaged, when my father and Giovanni, the bachelor, pulled us apart. To my mortification, I found that I had a hideous blue lump under my left eye. Now I have always been peaceful, even when young and have always looked upon violence as an evil thing. I had been striking up acquain-

tances with some of the people in the village and I
was very much ashamed to let them see that I had
been fighting. Therefore, after much solemn medi-
tation, I decided to tell everybody that I had fallen
down.

First I asked the foreman what the English for
falling down was. He told me, "faw don."

I began to repeat to myself, "faw don, faw don,
faw don . . ." It was evening and I was picking my
way down the icy road toward the town. Right outside the first houses two American fellows were quar-
relling, and I paused to watch and listen. One of
them was shaking his fist under the other man's nose
and saying, "You damn!" Somehow I forgot "faw
don" and as I walked away I was repeating "You
damn! You damn!". . . unconscious of the change.

The first man I met was an American brakeman,
who wore a collar on Sunday and whose acquaintance I esteemed greatly.

He greeted me, "Hello, Pat!" Everybody called
me Pat. "What's happened to you?"

"Me?" And I assumed an expression of sad innocence. "Me? You damn!" and I pointed to the
ground.

"What?" he exclaimed.

"Yes," I repeated in a louder voice, "you damn!
You damn!"

He laughed, said something and walked on, leaving me a little offended and grieved at his lack of
sympathy.

The same thing happened when I met a young

lady who worked in the yard office. And all around the place I went repeating my sad tale of "You damn!" When finally one man made me understand what I had been saying, I was so ashamed that I hurried straight home. And on the way I met Filippo, also angry, and we had another fight.

Our first four years in America were a monotonous repetition of laborious days. Everywhere was toil, yet they were happy years, for the foreman was kind and work was not so scarce; and monotony does not hurt when people are satisfied. While things seemed to be going so well some trouble that developed in our foreman's family caused him to leave hurriedly for Italy late in 1913. Still our gang kept together for one more year until the incidents came that finally separated us.

Everywhere was toil – endless, continuous toil, in the flooding blaze of the sun, or in the slashing rain – toil. In Hillsdale, Poughkeepsie, Spring Valley, New York, Falling Water, Virginia, Westwood, Remsey, New Jersey, Williamsport, Maryland, where the winding Potomac flows, Utica, New York, White Lake Corner, Otterlake, Tappan, Statsburg, Oneanta, Glen Falls, and many other places where we could find work, always as a pick and shovel man – that's what I was able to do, and that is what I work at even now.

Who hears the thuds of the pick and the jingling of the shovel? Only the stern-eyed foreman sees me. When night comes and we all quit work the thuds of the pick and the jingling of the shovel are heard

no more. All my works are lost, lost forever. But if I
write a good line of poetry – then when the night
comes and I cease writing, my work is not lost. My
line is still there. It can be read by you today and by
another tomorrow. But my pick and shovel works
cannot be read either by you today or by any one
else tomorrow. If I bring you to all the above mentioned places you will never be able to understand
all the work I was compelled to do, while I labored
there. You cannot feel from the cold roads and steel
tracks all the pains, the heartaches and the anger I
felt at the brutality of enforced labor. Yet we had to
live. We laborers have to live. We sell our lives, our
youth, our health – and what do we get for it? A
meager living.

NIGHT SCENE

An unshaped blackness is massed on the broken rim
    of night.
A mountain of clouds rises like a Mammoth out of
    the walls of darkness
With its lofty tusks battering the breast of heaven.
And the horn of the moon glimmers distantly over
    the flares and clustered stacks of the foundry.

Uninterruptedly, a form is advancing
On the road that shows in tatters.

The unshaped blackness is rolling larger above the
    thronged flames that branch upward from the
    stacks with an interwreathed fury.

The form strolling on the solitary road
Begins to assume the size of a human being.
It may be some worker that returns from next town,
Where it has been earning its day's wages.

Slowly, tediously, it flags past me –
is a tired man muttering angrily.
He mutters.
The blackness of his form now expands its hungry
    chaos
Spreading over half of heaven, like a storm,
Ready to swallow the moon, the puffing stacks, the
    wild foundry,
The very earth in its dark, furious maw,
The man mutters, shambling on –
The storm! The storm!

CHAPTER VII

My first real view of New York, the first time I actually realized the city, came in the summer of 1914 when I first visited Shady Side. Our job in Tuckahoe, New York, had stopped and I had come as a sort of advance agent for the gang in search of work. I came to the house of a couple of fellow townsmen. They boarded with some other Abruzzese in a shack perched on a high part of the Palisades.

I reached there Friday night. And when Saturday came one of my friends, Saverio, a very experienced man, took me and his companion to see the sights. "You cannot know the great city – not until I show you what it really is," he boasted. This was true, for on my first arrival in America I had hurried through New York as through some wild vision. And the immense powerful city had made little impression upon me. I have seen more gigantic and wonderful things in my dreams.

I had also lived for a few weeks in a cheap boarding house on Bayard Street with the gang when our job at Sparkshill, New York, was finished. But I was green then and my mind was yet unable to gather any impressions of the city, save that it was big, noisy and unintelligible. A dog whose eyes see a wonderful sunset, I suppose, feels about as much as I did at that time.

But a year made a good deal of difference and it was with a broadened vision that I came to Shady Side.

Saverio's companion was called Federico, a bronze-faced lad who had conceived a quick friendship for me in the short time I had been there. Dressed in our best, and looking rather handsome, in our estimation, we left the noisy house and climbed carefully down the face of the precipice on a narrow coiling footpath that leads into Gorge Road.

Gorge Road comes pouring like a stream from the cliffs and joins River Road. Dirty shacks and hovels are everywhere at the foot of the Palisades. On tiny terraces are barn-like houses clinging to the bare, stony slope, one above the other, filled hive-like with people talking, people arguing, people smoking and eating, singing and strumming guitars.

Slowly the last light drew from the strip of sky that glimmered between the cliffs of the Palisades and the looming masses of factories along the black river. Men and women, dirty, speaking a mixed jargon of Italian, Polish, Hungarian, English, were hurrying all about. Two husky laborers were appearing from the gloom of a factory door. One old Italian with golden rings in his ears was prodding some goats upward toward the terraced shacks. Children played everywhere.

"Saverio, my friend, you can't refuse a drink with us!" a voice came from a small shed-like house up above whose four windows glowed red with a new lamplight. Someone was atrociously playing a mandolin.

The three of us stopped.

Saverio excused himself. We had to go to New York. We were sorry with many thanks. And leisurely we began to saunter on through Shady Side to the ferry at Edgewater.

Shady Side is merely a factory town. It has nothing but factories and workingmen's shacks. How many of them are to be found all over the country! Towns of filthy hovels, towns of congested quarters and unhealthy conditions, all of them, little miniature East Sides and Mulberry Bends, scattered among the green stretches and broad open spaces of America. And over each of them, feeding upon them, looms the ever-present factory or mill. According to the higher concepts of life, these people seem to just barely live. But I know that they are no more unhappy than the nervous men and women whose lives consist of hurrying daily to and from gray apartment houses to gray offices. When I was in the darkness of ignorance, among them, a laborer and nothing else, I was happy.

In the gloom, now, the windows began to glimmer around us; the muddy road appeared soft and misty, the fumes that coiled down from the factories became ghost-like. A couple of drunkards staggered past and went tumbling into a saloon. It seemed as if each house on River Road had a saloon on the ground floor. And gambling and drinking were starting up, it being Saturday night.

"Look, here's an American girl who fell in love with our foreman and tried to have him arrested! Ha! Ha!" Coldly a flaming haired woman of questionable appearance and decorations passed us. I suppose she couldn't understand Italian – at least not our dialect. But she must have felt the "Ha! Ha!" deep in her heart.

Sauntering ahead we left behind the noisy teeming shacks of Shady Side and entered upon a long, dark, factory-haunted stretch of road that leads to Edgewater.

Saverio became critical, "This is a peculiar country. I can never understand these people in America and their cold ways. They will go to the funeral of their best friend and keep a straight face. I believe they feel ashamed if in a moment of forgetfulness they've turned to look at a flower or a beautiful sunset. Some of them talk good English, I believe."

But I was gazing about, pleased at the sky, the moon, the factories and the great illumined city beyond the river, which I remembered like a vague dream.

We reached the ferry house. Automobiles were swirling all about. Just barely dodging one we got on the boat. And soon, excited in expectation, I was gliding toward the city that appeared to be spreading nearer and nearer to us, gigantically.

Walking up a street that I afterwards found out was called Manhattan Street, we finally came upon a brilliantly illumined thoroughfare. I could hardly believe my eyes, it was so wonderful at first; and

Federico too was gazing around delighted. But Saverio, the Americanized, assumed a cold impersonal attitude.

We paused in front of a jewelry store. I noticed that some well dressed ladies were disgusted at our appearance and moved away quickly.

"Forty-nine cents for these watch chains," observed Saverio.

"How abundant and cheap is even gold in this wonderful place," I thought. Long and dreamily we gazed over the display of splendor. Finally as we moved away, Federico said, "I once bought one of my girls a fine gold bracelet. The only trouble was it began to rust after a few weeks and made a blue ring on her arm." We both sympathized with him, Saverio in a sardonic way.

We paused in front of another window. Again people edged away from us. And I heard some slurring remarks about "those foreigners."

"Look at this!" whispered Saverio.

Down the street came one of those women whose hideousness and folly no thickness of paint can hide. She had glaring yellow hair, hard irregular features, double chin, gray eyes and blood-red lips. With silks, plumes, furs, and other portions of slaughtered animals, she was the very incarnation of mankind's brutal vanity. Yet not one turned in disgust from this dazzling creature as they did from us.

Federico observed, "She looks like the demon himself."

I thought she must be a lady of the aristocracy

and told them so, at which both laughed. The over-adorned lady floated past with a sickening aroma of perfume. And we three walked happily along.

Right before us was that broad view more wonderful than anything I had ever seen. It was almost as wonderful as when a few years afterwards, from a train on Manhattan Bridge, I saw Brooklyn Bridge hanging over the river with nothing to hold it up in the middle.

To me this thoroughfare was a magic vista. Men and women crowded continuously out of that dazzling distance. Where did they all come from? And why their silence? Who had cast the spell over them all? How pale they all were, I thought. Weakly pale they all seemed, like sprouts of seeds washed up by the rain. Cars clanged and rumbled past, filled with rows of statue-like people who sat within, motionless, ignoring one another.

Nobody nodded good evening to me or to my companions.

We hovered outside a crowd, all looking at shoes. Then we passed on to a florist's store where there was a glorious display. It seemed as if these cold people made it a silly point of honor not to stop or glance at an array of lovely things like flowers. Not a man in the crowd had put a twig of sweet basil over his left ear as the men – real men – of our town do on summer evenings. However, a snickering young fellow and an insipid blond girl came to cuddle together and coo over the floral display. So I may have been wrong after all; for love, like death and night is a great leveller, even in a metropolis.

And we three walked on, wanderers in a magic show of forbidden splendor and beauty. And I thought of how lovely and yet repulsive this enchanted city was.

CHAPTER VIII

My visit to Shady Side was unsuccessful and I returned to my gang in Tuckahoe. Another one of us who had gone looking for a job – I believe it was our gigantic Andrea – succeeded in landing work for us at Ovid, N. Y., near Lake Cayuga. From there we went to New Branford, Conn., Melbourne, Mass. and West Pawlet, Vt. That winter the whole gang was again confronted by a period of idleness. It is always hard to find work for eight or nine men, even in summer. We fellow townsmen in this strange land clung desperately to one another. To be separated from our relatives and friends and to work alone was something that frightened us old and young. So we were ready to undergo a good deal of hardship before we would even consider breaking up the gang.

Nor was our enforced idleness a thing to look at with pleasure. For in that period the tiny sums that we might have been able to save would quickly vanish and we would soon find ourselves in debt.

It was a bad winter and we decided to come to New York from where we would sooner or later find another job. Meanwhile we tried to limit our expenses as much as possible during our enforced sojourn in the city. And naturally we lived in the slums where people of ill repute are not difficult to find.

One evening Matteo Rossi, our "quiet ace of hearts," happened to be expertly touring from one saloon to another for the purpose of finding the free lunch that best suited him. In one of these saloons he met a young man, also in search of free lunch, and they began to talk. This man had just arrived in the city, a stranger, and was fearful of New York.

Matteo never lacked sympathy and moral help for the unfortunate, and at times he even extended pecuniary aid. The stranger must have convinced him deeply, for by the end of the conversation, our fellow-townsman was ready to extend brotherly help to him. And after a few reciprocal glasses of beer with which they sealed their friendship, Matteo invited the young man to spend the night with us.

We were sitting in the dim living room on Franklin Street where we slept at that time. It was the house of an old Abruzzese woman who rented out a few dirty beds to us. The door was opened and in stalked Matteo with his new found friend.

"Here you can safely pass the night and as many other nights as you wish," explained Matteo as he introduced the stranger to us. He was a powerful looking young fellow of pleasing face and claimed to come from Campobasso, which is not far from our own section. There seemed to be no trace of shyness or suspicion in him, either.

When the old woman entered, he said he would not bother to pay for his bedroom every night, but would pay for a whole week in advance. This was a very unusual thing and startled us, for we only paid a day at a time, being liable to leave at any moment.

The old woman accepted immediately and going into the room where we slept pointed out a bed to him, on one side of which he could sleep. The stranger appeared pleased and going out bought a few cans of beer which we drank while talking about the old country and jobs and food. He was a clever young man and soon Giorgio Vanno, sensing a rival, began to attack him verbally. And much to our astonishment the stranger beat our champion at his own game of repartee.

We all went to sleep early that night, the stranger sharing a double bed with his new found friend, Matteo, and Andrea. Very early the next morning the young man rose, and quickly dressing in the gloom, went out. Since it was cold and our beds comfortable, we slept rather late in the mornings getting up at about seven. We talked a little about the stranger and all our comments appeared to be favorable.

That evening he came in a little after dark and throwing himself on the bed, said that he was very tired. We didn't do much talking either for most of us were gloomy at the prospects of a long period of idleness. Rumors had reached us that work on the highways and railroads was practically at a standstill. A war had started in Europe, we heard. Things were bad everywhere. And in the mind of each of us lurked the suspicion that we would never find work again, and would probably starve to death in this cold and extremely snowy country.

The next morning the young stranger again rose ahead of us and went out to work. We were still sleeping at the time and none of us heard him go except Antonio Lancia, who besides being a singer was also a sort of "vigilante" and was very seldom caught asleep during the early morning hours. The stranger had hinted to Antonio about the distance of his job, and how long he had to travel before he got there. Why should one get up out of a warm bed and without apparent cause prevent a man, because he is a stranger, from rising and going to work in the early morning hours? So the young man went, unopposed.

Six o'clock came and then seven, but Matteo was not up yet. It was now raining very hard, and was such a bad and disagreeable day that only one or two had risen. Most of us hesitated at the thought of going out to look for a job. And when we did get up we took our time, a thing which is very rare among us except during periods of enforced idleness.

While Matteo was busy snoring, the door was flung open and Filippo, who had just stepped out came rumbling in.

"Hey! Hey!" shouted the youngster, shaking his uncle by the shoulder, "Wake up! Wake up!"

Matteo immediately ceased snoring, rubbed his eyes slowly, and directed them toward the gentle intruder.

"Lend me a nickel, uncle," explained the lad. "There's a pushcart of very cheap bananas passing outside, three for a penny. I want to buy some."

Grumbling in a good natured way, Matteo began to look for his pocketbook in order to give his nephew the requested nickel. For a minute he sought in vain. The boy was at the window looking at the receding pushcart. I had just risen, and putting my hand in my pocket, happened to find a nickel, which I gave to Filippo.

Matteo turned to the lad and grumbled, "Do me the favor to go to the devil, both you, the bananas, those who produce them, and those who sell them." Then, turning to me, with a little change in his tone, "As soon as I get up and find my pocketbook among my clothes, I'll give you the nickel."

"That's all right," I said, "I don't need it. I am willing to wait a year for the return of this loan."

Again, for the second time, the pacific uncle fell a victim to the invasion of Morpheus. But, of a sudden, afterwards when he was released, he realized that it was long past the time to get up, and he began to put his legs outside the bed. He rose. He went into the kitchen where all of us used to wash in the mornings. After he had completely washed himself according to his methods, Matteo began to put some more clothes on himself until he had enough to enable him to go out. He filled his pipe with *spuntatura,* about the strongest smoking tobacco manufactured in America. He struck a match, and in a second, thick puffs of smoke began to come from him. Three big engines starting a long, laden freight train could hardly make more smoke than he did. All of a sudden he instinctively dug his hand in his trouser pocket seeking his pocketbook. And the smoke poured vehemently from his peaceful pipe.

"What the devil!" he dug his hands into his other pocket. Another curse, more emphatic than the first. Into the first pocket again, and then into his jacket, the thick searching hand went.

Matteo's eyes opened wide as a suspicious thought came into his mind.

We had turned curiously toward him at his exclamations and frantic movements. Quickly he yelled the news: his pocketbook with sixty dollars in it had vanished. This caused us all a great shock, for sixty dollars is rather a large sum of money.

Matteo was not a man to waste much time in lamentation. "Down in these quarters I found him, and down here I'll find him again," he muttered with a threatening glint in his dark eyes. We were very sympathetic and offered our aid in the ensuing search for the stranger. Matteo nodded and grumbled ominously. "I'll find him. And when I do he'll know it." Saying which the angry man instinctively clenched his fist and shook his huge forearm toward the window.

All that day Matteo spent prowling through the Italian section that spreads around Mulberry Street. Some of us as we wandered about looking for a job kept a sharp eye open for the thief, but without result.

That night Matteo waited in the house – for the return of the young stranger! Filippo, who was young, kept insisting that perhaps it was a joke. But of course no one came to amiably return the money and exhort Matteo's forgiveness.

When we awoke, early the next morning, Matteo was already gone. His persistency augured ill for the thief, and I myself knew that a blow from his fist was not a thing to be lightly received.

That afternoon I ran across Matteo on Mott Street, and having nothing to do, offered to join him in the search. We prowled around for an hour when of a sudden, on Bayard Street, he stopped. His face became red.

"There he is!" he whispered.

High up, enthroned, and oblivious of our gaze, the stranger was having his shoes shined.

As he calmly puffed a cigarette, he turned and his eyes fell upon Matteo. Up he sprang. Shouting a very vigorous word, Matteo leaped after him and caught him by the arm.

All at once three or four young men, confederates of the thief came to his aid. One of them threw me down from behind. I pulled him down after me, and we grappled in the gutter. Shouting and excited, the populace came around. Two others attacked Matteo.

With his free arm the stranger punched him. Matteo hit the thief full blast under the chin, thus chilling his ardour. And Matteo shook the well-dressed young man and punched him. And Matteo kicked one of the two who attacked him. And Matteo started to drag the thief after him.

Just then, fortunately for us, Andrea came running up. He knew nothing of the fistic art. But one blow of his in the stomach sent a confederate of the thief rolling across the sidewalk. Matteo was still gripping the forlorn thief and yelling, "Police! Police!" Some of the spectators had been glaring in a threatening manner toward us, but Andrea's huge size made them discreet. Meanwhile the gangster who was grappling with me glanced up and saw Andrea running toward us. Up he sprang and fled.

With Andrea and me as bodyguard, Matteo now dragged the repentant stranger toward the police station nearby on Elizabeth Street. A noisy crowd followed us on our march, during which we did not meet a single policeman.

At the police station Matteo cried his woes in broken English. The stranger glibly shouted, "Arrest this man! He hit me without cause! I don't know him!"

"He's a thief," growled Andrea.

The police captain began to look sternly at the four of us. We all tried to say something at the same time. The captain told us to shut up.

Systematically then he began to question us. The thief denied everything and vociferously demanded that we be placed under arrest for assault and battery.

The upshot of this all was that the young stranger was searched. An old pocketbook was found on him. Immediately Matteo claimed it. There were forty dollars in it, though the original sum had been sixty dollars.

"But how do you know this is yours?" sternly asked the police captain, while the prisoner wildly claimed that he had found the pocketbook.

Quietly Matteo told him where to look and lo! written in ink on the inside of the pocketbook was Matteo's name!

That settled the prisoner. Meanwhile the police captain sternly informed Matteo that he himself would have been arrested were it not for the finding of his name in the pocketbook. Matteo, grown silent again, grunted in vindicated fashion.

At the trial the thief, who was really a Calabrese, was found guilty and received a very heavy sentence – all of which came from his underestimating the determination of Matteo. These gangs in the slums prey rather safely on the poor timid immigrant laborers. Well, Matteo, though quiet, was anything but timid and the stranger made the mistake of his life when he mistook our "ace of hearts" for an easy mark.

CHAPTER IX

And still we went around asking for a job. As the weeks passed on our condition became critical. One or two, including Giovanni the hilarious, were past the end of their resources and were approaching a point where they could no longer hope for a loan even from kind-hearted friends. Each one of us went about, seeking work for seven or eight men. But so desperate had we become that we began to consider separating and finding work in several different places. It hurts the conscience of honest people when they have to live on borrowed money. We were ready to go anywhere and one of us even began to talk about Chicago.

One evening when we had the usual gathering to see if anything new had sprung up, Giorgio, the clever talker, who was perhaps our most assiduous searcher seemed to be affected by an unusual sense of humor.

"Work is the easiest thing to find," he began, laughing merrily.

We turned our gloomy downhearted faces toward him.

"What is there to prevent a man from working as hard as he wants?" continued Giorgio.

We really didn't consider it an appropriate occasion for such foolish remarks, and one of us, my father, I think, told him so.

Giorgio straightened up, and with a merry light in his brown eyes, said, "Don't be afraid. I have found a place where we can all resume our labors before the end of the week."

Our eyes brightened. We all shouted at once, "Is it true?" We had doubts when Giorgio said a thing, for he was very rarely serious.

Giorgio swore by all the saints, with his hand over his heart, that the problem of finding a job had been settled by him. He had found the job for us all, and our worries would soon be over.

That night we ate more heartily to celebrate our unexpected luck. What could our celebration consist of? Perhaps adding another soup to our "menu" and a five-cent bottle of beer.

When going to bed, we talked long about the job. Giorgio was not sure where it was except that it was in the south.

"The south?" said Andrea, "that is where oranges grow."

The cold wind was assailing our windows and we thought with awakened pleasure of a warm countryside.

"There are negroes in the south," added another.

My father remarked, "I wonder what the railroad fare will be." The others were unwilling to talk about such an unpleasant thing and turning around under their coverlets began to discuss the more agreeable aspects, such as the climate and the state of vegetation in the land of perpetual summer to which we were going.

With an indescribable restlessness we waited for the dawn. Someone got up at midnight asking what time it could be.

"Well," came Antonio's silvery voice, "don't fear. You won't miss tomorrow when it gets here. You won't miss it."

A couple of us were snoring. It was a very small room where the eight of us slept in three beds. We were all known to each other, or else we would surely have objected to sleeping with unknown men in a strange house.

It was not yet seven when we were all dressed. But according to Giorgio Vanno we would have to wait until ten o'clock before we could go to arrange for our departure. Filippo and I were anxious to look over the employment agency where he had found work, but Giorgio laughed at us and refused to tell us where it was.

In a happy mood, however, we went to an Abruzzese restaurant on Mulberry Street and told the proprietor about our good luck. He was a *paesano*, or fellow-townsman, who was feeding us on the mercy of credit. Almost with one voice we shouted the good news. He was very much pleased, for two evident reasons – one, that he would have to trust us no longer, and the other that he might soon begin to cash in what he had invested at the mercy of conscience. And I am sorry to say that some-one of us has not yet repaid his kindness.

After we had finished a leisurely breakfast, we looked anxiously at the clock. It was still early. However, we rose and instinctively followed the leash of our thoughts toward the "job-giving" place. We presented ourselves in front of the door half an hour before the appointed time, and began to walk back and forth in order to keep warm, for it was a cold, raw day.

As soon as the office door was flung open we timidly approached it and entered. A young man was putting out some glaring signs in Italian calling for *braccianti* or laborers. Inside, a pompous gentleman loomed in back of a wooden counter.

Giorgio whispered loudly, "He's the man who gives us the work."

Majestically, the man put on a pair of eyeglasses and scanned us. Other laborers, strangers to us, were crowding into the place.

Giorgio asked him how long we had to wait for a job, and how much it would cost to get to the place.

"It is like this," uttered the almost obese-looking man in a sonorous Neapolitan dialect, "you can start tomorrow if you want. The place is in West Virginia, which you may know, though I doubt it. I'll give you a letter of recommendation, and it will cost you five dollars for the fare – that is, if you all go together on one ticket, or else it will cost you eight dollars."

"Five dollars for each or for all?" asked Antonio.

Glaring at him in scorn the man turned impressively away toward a file cabinet.

High railroad fares are usually what keep laborers

near this hell-hole metropolis. Going to a distant job is a gamble. A man may pay a large part of his scanty savings for fare. And when he gets there he may find living conditions impossible and the foreman too overbearing. Perhaps he will be fired at the end of week. Where will he be then?

The obese gentleman mumbled almost to himself, "This is on the Cumberland Railroad."

We waited anxiously. All at once he wheeled about and thundered, "How many men are you in all?"

At this question everybody's heart nearly stopped beating. We felt sure that he asked us because he did not have enough work to occupy the whole gang. Each one said to himself, "Who knows how many men he wants? I may be the unlucky one who must be discarded."

Hesitating, Giorgio spoke up, "We are eight at present," and in his usual satiric way he added with feigned innocence, "but I can get you more good men, in case you want them."

"Fine! Fine!" exclaimed the portly dispenser of work. "This ticket calls for eleven men. That means three more. But be sure to get good people." Personally a man may be very bad, but as long as he spends more money than the rest in their camp stores, he will be listed as "good."

Immediately we set out on our task of hunting up three more "good" men in order to save three dollars each on one railroad fare.

Finally, down near the park at Mulberry bend we

ran across two husky acquaintances who were from a town not far from ours. We asked them if they wanted to go to West Virginia with us; we had two places open, luckily for them; their guardian saints had guided us to them.

Turning up his nose one of them answered, "You'll never get me to go down to that *casa du li diavel* in West Virginia, even if they give me five dollars a day."

The other said, if the trip was free he might be willing to come, even without his pal; but if money had to be disbursed in advance he was unwilling to take the chance.

So we continued walking through Mulberry Street, Franklin Street, Bayard, Worth and other illustrious downtown thoroughfares where we thought we might find "good" people who could fill the three empty places. It was a little hard because some had no money for the fare, and some didn't wish to part from New York believing that later they could find a job nearer town. Why should they go into the nether depths of the spacious Americas?

The fare was the terrible thing. There were plenty of men ready to work at anything, but they had no means of raising the five dollars. After we had visited three or four *paisani* restaurants and houses around Mulberry and Mott Streets we succeeded in finding three men who fitted all qualifications and who were anxious to work even in West Virginia.

So we all went to the old woman's house on

Franklin Street where we were still temporarily living – by paying fifteen cents per night – happy at
the thought that our gang was complete. We drank a
couple of cans of beer with our new comrades and
proceeded to get well acquainted. The first one of
them was called Teofilo. He had been a blacksmith
and, though small in size, had a tremendous arm development. Another was called Armando. He came
from Caserta and was a very handsome, bronze-faced
man. He had a bicycle and took it with him, thinking
that as the south was a warm place, he could use it
during his stay there. The third man, Nicolo, was tall
and lanky. We had some doubts of his ability to do
heavy work until he started with the pick and shovel.

Coming out we went into the employment office.
Each one of us gave the pompous gentleman five dollars for the fare, and handing us the ticket and letter
he announced that at three o'clock the same day we
could leave New York for our destined labors in West
Virginia. And we could arrive there in time to go to
work the following day.

We had about two hours to get ready. We all went
to get our bundles and our one valise in which we
had our common possessions. These consisted of pots,
four old tin plates, rather yellow-looking, some spoons
and forks for use in case we should ever dare to cook
macaroni. Years afterwards when I had learned some
words I named this same battered valise our "culi-
nary panoply." The rest of our armaments were a
needle, thread, an old pair of pants from which we
used to strip pieces of cloth for patching our clothes,

remnants of a linen shirt and numerous buttons taken from shirts and drawers which we had thrown away when they reached the unpatchable stage. We got our personal bundles ready, Andrea swung the heavy valise on his broad shoulder, and we set out toward the distant dock of the Pennsylvania Railroad. And there on our presenting the ticket we would be led, transported and conveyed to the land of sunshine and warmth.

Of course we walked, led by huge Andrea and Giorgio who looked very short beside him. We were light-hearted and talked loudly to one another. As we passed through the noisy streets many unhealthy, pale-faced inhabitants of the city glanced in disgust at the ragged clothes that covered our strong bodies.

While awkwardly crossing the crowded current of Broadway, one of our new men, Teofilo, was knocked down by the automobile of some hurried and careless inhabitant of this too-egoistic metropolis. We all ran to help him. A crowd collected. Teofilo rose to his feet. He was dazed but not much hurt at all – which was almost a miracle. This was very fortunate, for Andrea's face had gotten white and I knew that he would have sprung on that chauffeur and beaten him almost to death. Andrea had a glorious contempt for city people, especially for those who assume such superiority over us foreign laborers.

Picking up our things we hurried along toward pier 13. The catastrophe which had almost happened made us gayer and happier than ever. Good-naturedly we jested with Teofilo about his lucky name. On introducing himself to us he had seriously told us that anyone who was called Teofilo possessed seven golden blessings in his life. At present, we told him, he had only five blessings left, having already used up two of them, one when he met us, and the other when he escaped damage from the automobile.

Laughingly he answered, "Who knows? I may need all five of them in the place to which we are going."

In the land of summer and flowers? Unnecessary, we told him.

Finally we were in the train speeding through dull winter landscapes toward our new job.

CHAPTER X

It was during the night hours that we got off a local train and stood shivering and confused on a dark platform.

"Can this be the place?" we thought.

An icy sword-like wind assailed us. We shivered. It was bitter cold, worse than New York. And where were the oranges? And where the flowers?

The region was indistinct around us, its hilly distances glimmering faintly with long stretches of wet snow. Inside the small wooden station was a dimly lit room. In a body, we entered and presented our checks to the baggage master.

He shook his head.

There was no baggage for us. Perhaps it would arrive the following day. We were angered at the delay, for in our baggage were our warm quilts and mattress covers that we used to fill with straw or dried leaves on reaching a new place. We would have been considerably more angered at the time had we known where our poor baggage had gone. For there is another town in Pennsylvania also called Williamsport; and the carelessness of the baggage agent in New York had caused our belongings to be sent there.

Out we went, like a flock of sheep in the darkness where our feet sank at every step into wet sticky snow. It was beginning to rain as we started on our tramp toward the job which was about four miles away on the other side of the Potomac river.

Through the snow and rain we waded, hardly seeing our way in the dark. Each held his head down and trudged silently against the downpour which now came full-blast against us. Our clothes were absolutely soaked, like sponges unable to absorb another drop. As the cold rain fell it froze on the ground and we began to slip and slide. We had to walk the entire distance on railroad ties which were so slippery that each of us must have had at least a dozen falls before we reached our destination.

As we were crossing the Potomac on a long trestle the wind blew my hat into the water. A train rumbled toward us, its light flashing. We clung for life on the narrow space outside the track, but nothing happened save that Teofilo of the lucky name dropped his personal bag containing his most precious belongings into the Potomac.

On reaching the West Virginia side we again plunged into the hilly darkness. After we had trudged on for heaven knows how long, we saw the faint glimmer of lamplight through a small shanty window. We approached, hoping that it was the place we were seeking. But a fat negro who stepped to the door announced that we still had another mile to go before reaching the end of our journey.

On we went. Miles appeared very long that night. And finally, after a seemingly endless walk we reached the camp. Shining with the rain that had frozen to their black walls, five long shanties appeared in the dark. At one side was the camp store, a small shack where the commissary man sold bread, clothes, liquors and other necessities at the most exorbitant prices.

We knocked at the door of the first shanty. A man peeked out. At our request he slipped a jacket over his shoulders and came out to guide us toward the shanty where Mike the commissary man was.

On our entrance Mike was just opening a bottle of beer. He peered curiously at us. Four other men were playing cards around an empty beer keg which they used for a table.

Looking us over with fishy gray eyes Mike stepped out toward our party. Georgio Vanno explained who we were and Mike grunted for answer.

We announced our predicament, that we had no blankets or mattress covers and were wet to the skin.

He shrugged his shoulders, mumbling, "Too bad. But I can't help you. You may sleep in the next shanty where there is room for you." Saying which, he turned toward his beer bottle and smacked his lips.

We went out and hurried into the next shanty where only four other men were living at the time. Along the walls were broad shelves of pine boards on which we could sleep.

The driving wind shook the thin walls of the shanty which were merely composed of boards with tar paper nailed on the outside. Undecided, shivering, we all stood there. They had a stove in the place,

but no coal; nor was there a stove pipe through which
the smoke could pass out.

One of the four who was lying on the shelf turned
about under his warm blanket and grumbled that
we could get some soft coal at the boiler house.
When we finally succeeded in starting a fire, however, it was impossible to stand the gas given off by
the soft coal.

Without any appreciable success we tried to dry
our clothes. It was getting very late. And gradually
tiredness and sleep won us. Drearily we threw ourselves on the boards over which we had strewn some
dirty straw.

When we arose early next morning our muscles
were all stiffened and ached terribly. In order to lim-
ber ourselves a little we moved up and down the
shanty.

A frost had succeeded the icy rain and we felt the
wet of our clothes piercing our bodies like sharp
needles.

The commissary man came in and said that we
had better hurry out to work or we would get no
food whatever from his store. And standing he
glared about to see if anyone was sick or unable to
rise. Seeing us all up, he went rumbling on, and
returned after a while with the foreman who was
to boss us.

The creaking and cracked floor was strewn with
straw which had fallen from the shelves or "beds."
Straw covered our clothes and hair. The whole inside of the shanty with its forlorn occupants gave a

picture of moral wreck and bitterness. We were pigs in our sty.

This commissary man, Mike, though violent and ferocious, was really not so bad at heart. Once or twice he would, when drunk, threaten a few of the men with a rifle. But outside of that he was rather better than many others I have had the misfortune to know.

The commissary system prevails throughout this country. In its most extreme workings it results in perpetual peonage of the unlucky laborers who get caught. Usually the lure is high wages and free transportation to some distant locality. My own uncle, Giuseppe d'Angelo, was attracted to a place in Florida where he was held eight months before he was able to effect an escape. The food they gave him was vile and the living conditions were unspeakable. The laborers – white men – were guarded by ferocious negroes with guns which they used at the least excuse. And this in free America. No wages are paid, and the men are told that instead of expecting any they themselves are in debt to the company.

A commissary man contracts to furnish the company with laborers. In return he is given the privilege of running the camp store – an absolute monopoly most of whose profits go to men higher up. He also has a free hand over the men, firing, hiring, robbing and even preventing poor unfortunates from leaving.

The commissary man always tries to get acquainted with men who have a large number of friends among the workers and who can persuade them to go where he wants. This sort of man gets perhaps 15 or 20 cents more per day – which is considered an envied privilege, besides the fact that his board bill is always lower than anyone else's.

Each man has a small book in which are marked the prices of the objects he buys. The commissary man also keeps a book. And it is his book that counts, not the laborer's. If you try to save money and spend very little you will find when pay day comes that you are charged with as much debt as someone else who ate his fill. In the more decent places, where men are not slaves, the man who does not spend enough usually gets fired after a few warnings. A laborer is compelled to buy from the camp store at prices which would make a New York profiteer green with envy. And what they do receive after the commissary bill is deducted amounts to very little.

The foremen are helpless and subordinate to the commissary man. When work is scarce it is the married men who are the first to be fired, for the single as a rule spend more. And a man who drinks every cent he earns is considered a "good" man. The most welcome person is an organizer – not of unions – but of games. For during games the beer flows freely, for whoever loses must buy drinks.

And all this in free America!

We followed our new foreman down the road. We were by now auguring ourselves bad luck.

"Who knows how it will end?" muttered Antonio.

We thought of our lost baggage and our vanished

dreams of a sunny climate. Sheeplike we followed our foreman to where a large gang was already working. There were little engines called "donkey" puffing back and forth. A steam shovel was lifting a big rock caught in its iron teeth. Steam drillers were battering the stony bank alongside the railroad. Derricks were swinging the heaviest boulders about 20 feet above the ground with amazing ease. Now and then a Cumberland Valley Railroad freight train would pass by; then a coal train; then a passenger train.

All at once while we were approaching this orderly confusion a man came running toward us shouting and waving a red flag. The workers scurried under the cover. We stopped. There was a roar and half of the rocky bank flew up in a thousand pieces. None of us was hit though badly menaced. When everything which had gone up had finally come down, we timidly approached the shattered ledge of rocks. And without many ceremonies the foreman set us to work there.

Several weeks passed. We were dissatisfied with the place. Some talked of leaving. Some talked of staying a little while more. Rumors were reaching us of good jobs in other parts.

One day we were working on an embankment. A derrick was perched above us. We used it to lift big boulders into the cars that were pulled on the improvised tracks by the donkey engines.

There was a snap, a yell.

One of the guys or cables that held the derrick broke. Down crashed the enormous structure.

Shouting together we leaped away. There was a howl of pain, blood-curdling and piercing. We turned our startled eyes. Two men were pinned under the derrick. One of them was Teofilo, the other our huge Andrea.

It seemed almost the work of an instant that snapped the life of the smaller man. Andrea was still alive, though, his face twisted by agony. Teofilo stared off into infinity.

Quickly we all rushed together to lift the derrick. But we were too excited; and as we raised a ponderous weight, in spite of our taut muscles, it slid down the embankment. With a horrible grinding sound of flesh and bones it crushed the last life out of Andrea Lenta. We covered our eyes with our arms and groaned.

Within a few days after this fatal accident the gang broke up. We had lost all heart; work in that place was oppressive; we felt enslaved. And finally, discouraged and saddened by our loss, we decided to quit. Sadly we returned to New York.

One night shortly after our return my father announced to me that he was thinking of leaving for Italy. "We are not better off than when we started," he said, and asked me if I wished to go back with him.

I shook my head. Something had grown in me during my stay in America. Something was keeping me in this wonderful perilous land where I had suffered so much and where I had so much more to suffer. Should I quit this great America without a chance to really know it? Again I shook my head. There was a lingering suspicion that somewhere in this vast country an opening existed, that somewhere I would strike the light. I could not remain in the darkness perpetually.

My father was much saddened, for I was unable to make him understand the thoughts that were vaguely moulding in my mind. And he went away from me, a broken-hearted man.

Matteo and Giorgio returned to Introdacqua. Antonio went out west and I have never heard of him since. The others found jobs near New York, but gradually drifted away. And of the original gang I have only seen Filippo once or twice.

I was left alone.

While wandering around New York I ran across a fellow-townsman, an older man called Gaetano. We kept together for company's sake, and tried to get a job in Albany, Troy and New Haven. Fully discouraged we returned to New York.

Toward the end of January we met a man from Shady Side who was a friend of my new companion. This man was a foreman on the Erie Railroad yard about two miles south of Fort Lee ferry. He told us that the pay was too small – it really was: $1.13 per day. During the preceding summer our wages had been $1.85 and we were terribly shocked at the news. In spite of all shocks, however, we had to submit and indeed considered ourselves lucky to find any kind of work that terrible winter.

We went to live in a box car located in the center

of the yard where a few men were already staying. It was a broken down affair which scarcely protected us from the rain. In winter frost and ice were near my ill-kept bed. My best blanket which my mother had made for me and which had peregrinated through America with me, was now divided into many useless pieces.

Living in the box car we were always handy in case there should be a wreck or other trouble. We were liable to be called out at any hour – usually in the middle of the night. In spite of rain, snow, sleet and icy wind, we had to work until the wreckage was removed and the damaged tracks repaired.

That was our work; handling and carrying wet ties on our shoulders, now and then stumbling on the rough ground of the unlit yard, and cursing just to appease our pains – with the heavy ties and rails on our shoulders and the slippery ice under our feet. That was our work. All around was noise and confusion; trains piling on trains – cars creeping smoothly at you in the darkness, bells, toots. While I was there two men were caught under a freight car, several were smothered under coal in the coal dumps, one suffocated in the steam house. It was a war in which we poor laborers – Poles and Italians – were perpetually engaged.

The accident in the coal dump made a vivid impression on me. And I tried, long after, to describe its effect in the following poem:

ACCIDENT IN THE COAL DUMP

Like a dream that dies in crushed splendor under
    the weight of awakening
He lay, limbs spread in abandon, at the bottom of a
    smooth hollow of glistening coal.
We were leaning about on our shovels and sweating,
Red faced in the lantern-light,
Still warm from our frenzied digging and hardly
    feeling the cold midnight wind.
He had been a handsome quiet fellow, a family man
    with whom I had often talked
Of the petty joys and troubles of our little dark
    world;
In the saloon on Saturday night.
And there he was now, huge man, an extinguished
    sun still followed by unseen faithful planets,
Dawning on dead worlds in an eclipse across
    myriad stars –
Vanished like a bubble down the stream of eternity,
Heedlessly shattered on the majestic falls of some
    unknown shores.
And we turned slowly toward home, shivering,
    straggling, sombre –
Save one youngster who was trying to fool himself
    and his insistent thoughts,
With a carefree joke about the dead man.
Snow began to fall like a white dream through the
    rude sleep of the winter night,
And a wild eyed woman came running out of the
    darkness.

CHAPTER XI

OMNIS SUM

On the Calvary of thought I knelt, in torment of
    silence.
The stars were like sparks struck from the busy
    forge of vengeful night.
The sky was like a woman in fury
Disheveling her tresses of darkness over me.
It seemed as if the whole universe were accusing me
Of the anguish of Deity.

When a laborer leaves one locality for another, he
always does so for some fancied betterment and not
with the idea of touring the country. There is nothing for him to see. And always, the lure of advantage is changed after the first few days into disillusion
and remorse. For wherever he goes there are hovels,
hard work and brutal foremen – and that feeling of
autocracy over him which he probably never knew
before and which makes him bestial and uncon-
sciously fatalistic.

In 1916 while all the other companies were paying good wages our own beloved railroad, the Erie,
was persistent in allowing us $1.50 per day. We asked
for $1.75, which was reasonable and less than what
other places paid. But our demands, though honest,

were indignantly rejected and the whole gang left in a body. In those days when work was rapidly picking up after a long slump, it was a matter of each man finding the very best he could. My case was typical: a long lay-off the previous year had left me in debt. And now there was a chance of making money. I was lured by the $2.25 per day promised on the state roads in Northern New Jersey, and went there alone. I spent all the money I had for the fare.

There were many various gangs working in the place: stone-breakers, stone-drillers, excavators, concrete workers and others, each with its own foreman. There were men loading stones of various sizes newly broken, on wagons; steam-rollers puffing along; gangs laying out first large stones, then smaller, and then sand. Over everything they put on tar and a covering of powder which we called "fine stuff."

I succeeded in getting work with the concrete gang. The road was progressing rapidly. There were rivulets over which little concrete bridges were required. Having no mixer for the concrete we had to mix the sand, stones and cement with our shovels right on the spot. And here came some of our hardest work, especially hard, as it was summer. On some of those cloudless days when the sun blazed down on us we would be carrying dusty bags full of heavy cement on our shoulders continuously. The dust mixed with the sweat beneath, burning the shoulders and itching. Very often after I had wiped my cheeks and around my neck with a dirty handkerchief I had to spread it out on the grass to dry while

I staggered along through the flaming sunlight with my load. When dry the cement made the handkerchief appear petrified.

And the mixing. The foreman was getting angry that I wiped my face while the others worked bowed with the sweat pouring down over them. He snarled that it was just an excuse for raising my bowed body from the continual toil. This foreman's name was Domenick. He spoke in a weird Calabrese dialect and cursed always. He was a big broad-shouldered man, but his dry features were irregular and looked dissipated and his eyes were bloodshot. There was no appeal for one of us from his autocracy and he knew it. He had his spies in the gang and tyrannized over us – this foreman of the concrete workers. His threat of firing always awoke in us visions of aimless wanderings and dark months without jobs. And deep in his heart a man hates to go around begging for a job to be greeted with a sneer or a turned shoulder. Well, this foreman made us understand that in order to straighten our backs even a little, we needed a better excuse than that of wiping the sweat from our faces even though burning with cement dust. We said nothing, but bowed lower, while he stood straight watching us all the time. That was his job.

We had to dig foundations for these small bridges or "culverts." And always we found water; my feet were wet practically all the time. One day the foreman ordered us to go down into a short trench or foundation and make it deeper. The bottom was a deep pool of brown water. Most of the men had rubber boots; I had none. I hesitated.

The "boss" who was beginning to dislike me shouted harshly, "If you want your ten hours put down in the time book you'd better go down and dig; and hurry up about it." And down I went.

Often I'd try to put a piece of wood or flat stone under my feet; but usually the stone sank in the mire or my feet slipped away while working. So I invariably got wet. Rain or sunshine we had to work ahead; for our tyrant was that sort of man whom the contractors call "an excellent and efficient foreman."

One day while we were finishing one of those small bridges, it began to rain. The planks leading to the top of the foundation on which we had to climb were more vertical than horizontal. It was a steep climb up any time. And the rain rendered it more difficult by making the planks slippery. My job was to push wheelbarrows full of concrete up to the top of the foundation and dump the mixture down into the wooden forms. This was continuous and very hard work, for as soon as I returned an empty wheelbarrow, another full one greeted me. It was almost impossible to push a high-heaped wheelbarrow on the inclined slippery planks. I was going up with one not quite so full when the foreman shouted something to the men below.

Coming back I found the second wheelbarrow filled up to the brim. I paused. The foreman came running up, hot-faced. I said the load was too heavy to safely handle on the wet planks.

Grasping the handles he raised them and looking fiercely back, shouted, "Heavy, is it?"

"Well," I remarked, "anybody can do that. But look where I must go with it."

"I'll show you!" and he cursed. He started pushing the heavy wheelbarrow up toward the woodwork. But his feet began to slip a little and he saw that there might be danger for him. So he stopped and said, "But why should I go there? I'm the foreman. What do you think I have you here for?"

Meanwhile some of the bolder laborers, recognizing my right, began hurriedly to take off a few shovelfuls from the top of the overladen wheelbarrow. But the boss, cursing and threatening to fire the whole lot of them, made them put it back. And he ordered me to go ahead with the load. Without another word I bowed myself – a weakling under the force of necessity. The injustice of it split my thoughts like lightning, and I realized that a fire was smoldering in me. But what could I do? Rain was falling heavily. Not much time was given to decide. Almost without knowing it I found myself pushing upward a top-heavy wheelbarrow. While reaching near the top my feet slipped and I lost my balance. The wheelbarrow dropped down into the foundation. Wildly I threw out my hands and propped myself against the woodwork in order to avoid an inevitable fall. A rusty nail pierced my right hand. And I shrieked. Blood began to come out from both sides of my hand.

The foreman came running up. "Get out, you

fool!" he shouted, "you can't work here any more!"
And I couldn't.

All wet, tired, with bleeding, aching hand, I went
back to the "shanty." My hand began to swell. I
didn't know what to do. There was a small village
further down the road but no drug store. There was
only a grocery store that had peroxide. So I went
down there through the rain, purchased a bottle and
hurried back to medicate my hand. In the dark
shanty there was an old stove but not lit. I could
not dry my wet clothes. There was not even a good
place where I could hang them out for the night.
Outside it was still raining. I hung my dripping jacket
near my wooden bed – a bed made of two boards
nailed together. Some hours passed without my eating anything because I didn't feel much like eating.
But even if I had been hungry, there was nothing
more in the place except a loaf of stale bread and a
piece of the cheapest and almost uneatable "Italian" salami made in America. In that condition, and
feeling a repulsion toward an undesired food, I went
to bed with an empty stomach. Now I began to be
restless and felt the full pain of my wounded hand.
My mind was dark. I felt like a hurt dog who slinks
off to some corner where it can lick its wounds in
silence.

Then the rest of the gang came straggling home
through the downpour. They all made noise, and
the chilly air of the shanty became foul with the
sweat that steamed from them. One began to start a
fire in the stove. A couple were arguing. There were

shouts; and smoke filled the shanty. Some went to get food. There was frying in fat. After eating, one of them came over to ask me how I felt.

It was past midnight, but my eyes had not yet been closed. Everything was silent now save the beating of the rain outside and a sharp measured drip on the floor near the foot of my bed. The fever that was beating my wounded hand seemed little better, and sleep began to intensify. By about two o'clock in the morning I must have fallen asleep.

By five o'clock same of the men began to stir. They rose, yawned and spoke, and set about preparing their breakfast and some lunch to be taken on the job. Some whistled. An old fellow sang. Somebody was cursing outside that the wood was too wet and he couldn't get the fire going.

From a corner came a shout, "How is the weather? Is it worth while getting up?"

Someone shouted back, "It doesn't look so bad today. You'd better get your lunch ready."

About ten minutes to six a few started for the job. It was still quite dark, the sky showing through the open door in a gray turmoil of clouds and mists. Others began to leave, and by a quarter after six there was nobody around me. For a while I remained alone in that dim barn-like place. Then instinctively, in spite of my wounded hand, I felt the need of going to work and I too got up. Hurriedly I dressed and ran just as fast as I could in order to get to the job on time. I was hoping that foreman might have got over his anger and would give me some other work that I could do.

It was just about one minute after seven when I came running up breathlessly. The last man had not yet picked his tools.

The foreman eyed me steadily and then said, "You are too late. If you want to work come at noon."

"But listen," I said quietly, "why must I lose five hours? If I am too late for seven o'clock can't I start at eight?"

He insisted, "No! I said noon." And he turned his broad back to me. From the tone of his voice and his demeanor I could see that, king-like, he had placed himself up in a tower of caprice – this ignorant man who had power over men. So, without adding any more futile words I did the only thing possible; slowly I walked back to the shanty and waited for noon.

Noon came. A distant whistle blew beyond some trees and then died out as if it were the last breath of silence. The sky had cleared and only a vague mist was blazing around the sun. Again I started out for the job, walking quickly through the throbbing brightness of the day. My wounded hand was very much swollen; I had tightened a handkerchief soaked in peroxide around it.

I was badly in need of money and realized that I had to submit under any circumstances. As soon as it was time to resume work I planted myself meekly before Domenick.

But he, without any human consideration, said, "Take your shovel, go there with the others and mix the concrete!"

"But, no," I interrupted gently, "I came here to

see if you have any job that I can do." And I held
out my swollen, bandaged hand. "Will you give me
a job as water-boy? I can do that easily."

Apathetically he answered, "No. If you can't use
a shovel then go home and stay there until your
hand is healed. That's all." And with that, he went
back to his work of watching the gang of workers.
For an instant my thoughts were in a whirl. That is
why many foremen carry revolvers on the job. Then
slowly I left the spot and began to plod my way
home, if I could call that hovel "home."

I still remembered vividly – everybody remembered it – the heart-breaking times of the previous
year, the long days out of a job when indefatigable
search was only rewarded by the repeated "No, no."
I was without money and in debt; otherwise I
wouldn't have cared so much.

Night and inevitable darkness came, and the tired
workers returned home sullenly, like wild beasts toward their den. They divided themselves into many
groups, and each group began its own fire on the
bare field in front of the shanty. I sat on a boulder
quietly watching them, my wounded hand on my
knee. Every now and then I would look at it ten-
derly like some mongrel who gently licks its wounded
paw.

Now all the various fires began to glimmer and
crackle, and the tongues of bright flames licked the
velvet night. Some men were coming duskily with
wood; some went for water; there was the welcome
sound of pots; one man in each group chopped wood

in the glow of the hungry fire. There were also a few among us who had no group to co-operate with and would hardly be getting our half-cooked supper before half past ten. And by then we would be so tired that with the pot still boiling on the two stones and the steam pouring up we would probably be half asleep. And many a man has lost his supper because the fire galloped along freely while he nodded. And finally when the smoke and bad odor awoke him the supper is hopelessly burned in the dirty pot. And many a time, tired and mad, a man has gone to sleep without eating.

The night was beautiful. The stars were like exquisite, happy, living spirits giving their bright laughter to the silent night. A few were beginning to munch their food. The rest were moving about or waiting. In spite of the soft weather they all seemed to be in ill humor. The night before, when coming into the shanty all wet, shouting and stamping about, they had been much more lively. And though not one of them said a word, it seemed that the balmy summer night had awakened deep in their hearts the vision of another land, lovely and balmy and calm. A land that doesn't know any such things as foremen, in small towns where one is never among strangers and people help one another.

While I was sitting there, along came a young fellow called Tony. He was the one who had asked me how I felt the night before, in the shanty. He was short and slender and had bright black eyes and wrinkled face when he smiled. Said he, "Why don't you go and see some other foreman for a job?" There were several scattered here and there each of them taking care of a different phase in the construction. These foremen boarded at various farms conveniently near the work. They got good wages and bonuses for watching us. They also put in time for us all and short-paid the men. Their food was ready for them at night and their beds were soft and clean. And we who did the work slept uncleanly in human sties.

I decided to follow Tony's advice, and started out immediately.

As I went down the road the moon arose and shone on the exquisite summer night. The warm wind came soft and steadily, the road gleamed delicately, and on the embankments to one side the cascades of dried loam appeared of fragile gold. There were not many trees around, but long stretches of indistinct fields lifting into nowhere.

Just then I noticed, stumbling a short distance ahead of me the big foreman Domenick who had caused me so much trouble. He was probably drunk. He had struck up a friendship with a woman in another farmhouse and was probably returning from her place. Immediately a fury such as I had never known before flared up in me. I hurried. Then I paused. But I have always abhorred violence. And a sudden pain from my swollen hand streaked through my being.

Just then, as I hesitated I felt a hand on my shoulder, not heavy, and gently laid. With a start I turned. It was old Michele who worked with some other foreman. He was also an Abbruzzese, but he came from the bright Adriatic coasts where groves of lemons and oranges grow right to the edge of the cliffs that overhang the sea. He had not spent his young manhood in this wretched endless labor and degradation among strangers. And his eyes were bright as if in them were still gleaming the hopes of youth. But now he was old and he liked drink.

He called me by name, "And where are you going, boy?" He was an intelligent man and spoke in excellent Italian. He had worked on our gang for a week and often mentioned Dante whom I thought was an ancient king. But now, old, the foreman took him on more in pity than anything and because he could talk so nicely to them.

I showed Michele my wounded hand and told him my predicament. He now spoke in his soft Abbruzzese dialect that is so much like ours of the uplands, "Boy," he said, "a stupid world drove nails through other hands – other hands."

I didn't know what he was talking about. But at times afterwards the image of that aimless old man has come before me like a frightful specter and at times like an alluring hope.

He laughed and took a hearty leave of me. I hurried along. Domenick had long since disappeared. Some lights of the houses gleamed around a turn of the road. There was a living haze around. And suddenly I felt the voluptuous summer night embracing me mother-like, and amazing with love. And my heart ached for home. And I dreamed of the moonrise over the rugged peaks of the eastern mountains when in among the black pinnacles are cups of molten silver overflowing and everybody looks up without knowing why.

But I was out to get a job. I shook my head at all these useless thoughts, and continued my way. Finally I reached the first farmhouse. The foreman came out. He told me his gang already had a waterboy, and shut the door. The second one, on a more distant farm, said that his gang was too small to have one. This was a lie. Completely discouraged, I decided that it was useless to go and see the third foreman who lived further down the long endless road. So I returned to the sty. I felt lost.

When I crossed the well-worn threshold one of the men put down his pipe and asked, "Hello! did you get any place?" He was a loud-mouthed, but good-natured Neapolitan whom I hardly knew.

I shook my head.

There was another older man sitting on a box near the door, and he asked, also in Neapolitan, "What has he been looking for?" This man was a stranger to me.

The first fellow, who must have been quite familiar with him, turned and said loudly, "Why I'll tell you. First of all you foremen and bosses seem to think that you are gods and kings around here. Why, look at this lad; yesterday he got hurt on the job; and his hand is still bleeding and swollen. He wants a light job that he can do; and nobody wants to give him any. That dog Domenick over there told him that he must wait until his hand is healed so he can use a shovel. But if he came out here without money – what the devil is he going to eat in the meanwhile? You know yourself how a man can be in a hole at times."

So I discovered that this stranger was a foreman in the excavation gang. He seemed not so bad as the others. He had just dropped around to have a chat with his fellow-townsman, luckily for me.

"Well, boy," he began half sympathetically, "come over to my gang tomorrow morning, south of here."

The next morning I arose feeling a little more certain and encouraged. I removed the handkerchief from my hand and put on a cleaner one, I tried to fry a couple of eggs in an old greasy pan. Then I took a half loaf of stale bread, split it, weakly, and put the half-fried eggs in between the pieces. I searched around for a piece of paper but could find none. I was in a hurry, the men were leaving, and I had to go further than they. Quickly I drew my other handkerchief from my pocket. It was still dirty with the blood that had oozed from my hand the day before. I wrapped the pieces of stale bread and the two fried eggs in it. And I took it with me as my lunch for noon.

So I worked every day with this new gang, carrying pail after pail of water to the men, who drank like mules. I had to go far off for the water and was unable to shift the heavy pail from one hand to the other. At times I had to pause on my way back; but this foreman seemed to be a little more considerate than the other, though he had his defects.

I worked there for about two weeks. My hand was not yet well healed. Then came the fortnightly pay-day. We were all waiting eagerly and thinking of the hour when the automobile with meats and vegetables would pass and we could buy something good. But when the usual hour for our money approached the pay-master failed to appear. An hour later one of the foremen who looked anxious, announced that the contractor had sent a telegram saying that he could not come that day but would be around to pay us about a day or two later. The approval was unanimous. We all went back to work happily, and eager to finish out that day like excited children waiting for a holiday.

About three o'clock in the afternoon the next day we saw a crowd getting together down the road. Someone came running up saying that another telegram had come. We all hurried over, the foreman first. The superintendent was there, white-faced. He read the telegram to us; then he explained that the contractor had gone bankrupt and that we didn't need to work out the day. The foremen crowded around him and started a hot argument.

Then, we all struck in despair. Like a flock of betrayed sheep we returned to the huge, barn-like shanty foolishly questioning one another. What could we do?

Some who had money or could get a loan returned to New York. Others went around begging the farmers nearby to give them work for the necessary fare. And I was there without money, and with a wounded hand, feeling full remorse for having made this newest change from my previous place.

But first, while most of the men were cursing eloquently a few of us had to sit down and laugh at one another.

CHAPTER XII

That night I lingered a long time outside the shanty, thinking. And darkness made the vast solitudes of heaven populous with stars.

At first my mind was turbulent.

And I thought to myself, "Why, I am nothing more than a dog. A dog. But a dog is silent and slinks away when whipped, while I am filled with the urge to cry out, to cry out disconnected words, expressions of pain – anything – to cry out!"

I looked around. I felt a kinship with the beautiful earth. She was like some lovely hardhearted lady in velvets and gaudy silks – one whom we could gaze at in admiration, but never dare approach. I felt a power that was forcing me to cry out to this world that was so fair, so soft and oblivious of our pains and petty sorrows. Then I had to laugh to myself. "After all," I thought, "what are my tiny woes to the eternal beauty of those stars, of these trees and even this short-lived grass?"

For a long time I paced the soft green in front of our shanty. Then I entered. The men inside were grumbling mournfully to one another, barely visible in the gloom. I had resigned myself to my fate. I was a poor laborer – a dago, a wop or some such creature – in the eyes of America. Well, what could I do?

Nothing.

Thereafter, for a long while until my numbed soul was again awakened, my prime interests were food and jobs. First of all I had to escape back to headquarters in New York. My credit was very bad.

I left the shanty with a couple of others; and we began to trudge aimlessly down the long road. At several farmhouses we paused to ask for work. None of the farmers seemed to care to give us any.

"What are you going to do?" asked a young bright-faced lad.

"Walk," grumbled my other companion, a Sicilian.

And walk we did. That night we slept in a most beautiful country side. But the mosquitoes and the gathering damp prevented our admiring the splendor of the broad starlit night.

Rising a little stiff-jointed the next morning we walked on. We were hungry; for a drink of water at a clear spring had not done much to soothe us. We had a little money between us, and on reaching a placid hamlet nestled amid soft green hills we made a quick run on the general store.

And who should be conducting the store but a *paisano* of mine! We shook hands long and vigorously and in a few minutes I was giving him a detailed account of everything that had passed in our village from the time he had come to America to the day, years later, when I left.

This good fellow-townsman of mine made the three of us sleep in his house that night. In real beds, too. And the next day he even loaned us the fare for New York, which I dutifully returned in time, as I hope my two companions did.

Back again to the railroad yard in Shady Side I went, humbly begging for a job. Fortunately for me, they needed men. And so it was that after my disastrous trip, I was again an inhabitant of our old box car.

Little by little a few other fellow-townsmen drifted back from unsuccessful jobs, and our original gang was in a way re-established.

Strange to say, I had become light-hearted after my troubles. Foremen would shout at me, and I laughed as soon as their backs were turned. I didn't care. I had resigned myself to the gradual eking out of my life. Work and food.

Up on Hudson Heights, on top of the Palisades, was a boarding house kept by a *paisana*. And there I would spend the evenings, joking and fooling. I walked up and down with a broad smile on my face. And it was just by accident, and from this same sense of joking that my life took an upward turn.

First of all, a crowd of Mexican laborers were brought up from the south to work with us in the yard. At first they were kept separated from us, living in long shanties. But gradually a general mingling of laborers took place and we fraternized wonderfully with them. And I found some of them real gentlemen. There was one, a wiry young man, who had been with Villa and had been taken prisoner by the Americans. Besides Spanish he could speak a strange Indian language that sounded very queer to me. That winter he and another older man came to live in our box car and our quarters, already crowded, became packed. They were lively fellows and would sing and play on a discordant guitar. Then at times the older one, Don Tomas, would start off reminiscing and put us all to sleep with his monotonous semi-comprehensible stories.

I began to learn some Spanish from these two Mexicans. The younger one received a Spanish weekly from some town in Texas. To my amusement he would sit hours at a time reading it. Little by little I became interested in the paper, and tried to pick out words that were like Italian. I had gotten to think of a newspaper as something to start a fire with or to wrap objects in. But now I began to read again – very little at first, I must confess. Somehow, I found English more to my liking than Spanish. And about once a week I even bought an English newspaper to look at. There was very little in them that I could understand, even though I spent many a puzzled hour trying to decipher the strange words. When I did learn a word and had discovered its meaning I would write it in big letters on the mouldy walls of the box car. And soon I had my first lesson in English all around me continually before my eyes.

One day a friend of mine who was a bartender in one of the many saloons that lined River Road took me to an Italian vaudeville show in a theater on the Bowery, New York. Included in the program was a short farce. I heard it and decided to myself that I could do better.

I went home and tried to write something after work. I began it in Italian, but unable to manage the language, on a sudden thought I decided to attempt it in English. After a few Sundays of hard work I had about three closely written pages of the most impossible English one could imagine. In triumph, I showed it to a couple of brakemen. They laughed long and loud. There was some doubt whether it was the jokes or the manhandled English which caused their hilarity. However, I gave myself the benefit of the doubt, and agreed with myself that I could write English.

Though I have long since burned most of these "prehistoric" attempts at English, I still have a few among my papers of which the following is an example:

A farmer had not bean in this city very long beefore he falled in love with sumthing. And this sumthing happen to be a wooman whoo disliked him just as passionately he liked her. Now, please do not think that this tuirns out to be a joke. Farther from it. This is a seerious story in witch throbs the most violent of human passions. The life of an unfortunate farm swolled up by the whirlpulls of evil. Revealing the futile struggles of a mother who fites to save her son drunkard by liquor which he had not yet drunk. He was like a drunken staggering alung the city streets and falls in some undignfied gutter out of which he emerges with his face embellished by mud and clothes

*smelling with heretofour unknown perfumes, made
out of the too old manure and many other effective
ingredients pertaining thereto.*

*He knelt beefore the wooman he lovd. Being
largely dispose to obesity (fatness) whenver she moved
away which she did it on purpose – he would go
after her (walking) on his knees. Most people become
eloquent when drunken or in love and this farmer
was not therefour exseption, "I love you" be begined,
"I love you so much. I love you! Please come near!
come nearer. You are my hope, my quween, my all!
You are like a goddes beefore witch I am never tired
of kneeling. You are the most beautful wooman in
the world you are moor beautful then beauty. More
beautful then one of our newly washed pig!" she went
way and he called her back "At least help me to git
up if you dont want marry me." She went and he had
a hard difficult job to get up.*

So I began to write jokes in "English," most of them
of my own invention or paraphrased from some
paper. My jokes became known around the yard as
great curiosities and things to laugh at. Several good-
natured lads who worked there even brought me
writing paper so that I could put down a few jokes
for them. The things I wrote were not refined at all,
but only of the type for my class of people.

Later, when I had learned to manage the English
language a little better and could write with some
degree of clarity, I put a prize of five cents on some
good jokes. That is, if they could keep a straight face
while reading a little collection of jokes that I presented them I would give them a nickel. But of course

they always refused the nickel. Thus was my first climax in the role of English author.

One day I bought a small Webster's dictionary for a quarter (second-hand, if not third), half torn. But I thought I had gotten a treasure for the price. And I proceeded to memorize it.

Thereafter I was continually going around the yard using the most unheard-of English words. But, insistently, I made them understand what I meant by spelling each word or writing them on a railroad tie.

From that time on I was continually asking questions and writing jokes and riddles – which were for me the heights of intellectual attainment.

One glorious winter night I was coming back toward the box car from a trip to Hudson Heights. With me were a couple of brakemen who were on a night shift and were going to work. They were young light-hearted American lads, always ready to joke with me.

I looked up. The sky was thick with stars. I remarked, "The stars are marching over the deep night. With whom are they going to war?"

"Eh? With whom . . . ?" they asked.

"With the emperor of Eternity."

"And who is he?"

"Death," I said.

They both laughed and took pains to make me understand that I was crazy. I walked ahead to my box car.

Shortly after this I began to project – ambitiously – a heart stirring tragedy. There was a small hall in back of one saloon on River Road owned by a Hungarian whose daughter I often spoke with. They were not bad people either, and she had beautiful blue eyes. Vaguely I made plans for producing a soul-rending show there, and charging admission, and making a good deal of money. Of course, I was to be the author of the sad play.

Now, just because I knew so little about the city, I determined to put my scene in the great metropolis. And the play was to start with a poor outcast who had to sleep in the subway. But when I sat down to write the speech of this poor being whose rest is disturbed by the rumbling trains, I didn't know what to say. Accordingly, I decided to investigate and spend a night in the subway, which I did very successfully in the matter of sleep. And I never wrote the sad tragedy, either.

But work, continual, hard, fatiguing work, made my attempts at writing few and short lived. I always was and am a pick and shovel man. That's all I am able to do, and that is what I am forced to do, even now. Work with my arms.

Wrecks in the yard were a daily occurrence. I could hardly concentrate my mind, when a man would come shouting, "All out! A wreck!" in the tunnel or away down the tracks toward the sugar refineries. Out I would have to go. And in a few minutes I would be starting long spells of intense, hurried labor to clear away the wreckage or repair the damaged tracks, in the red glow of flickering lanterns.

The superiority of my English was first recognized by the Italian laborers of my gang. Then brakemen and conductors who were practically all Americans began to notice me. And finally rumors of my accomplishments reached even the yard officials. I became quite celebrated in the Shady Side yard of the Erie Railroad as "that queer Italian laborer."

Then a group of young brakemen began a campaign to put down my little local fame. What they did was to bring new and difficult words every morning for me to define. Usually they would come about half an hour before working time, and cornering me would ask the meaning of some difficult word. If I could answer, all was well and they kept judiciously quiet for the rest of the day. But if I failed, then they would make it hot for me.

When noon came they would call me over to the space in front of the office where clerks, yard officials and girls were. And there they would, with plenty of noise, try to show me up to those who liked me.

But their efforts and mental ambushes were all useless – as useless as I could make them. One day they brought me before the whole crowd just to have me ridiculed, perhaps because they were high school lads. They gave me five words to define and I only knew the meaning of three. Throwing up their hands they began to proclaim themselves victorious.

But I calmly gave them two words that they had never heard of. Then I bet them that I could give them ten words and two more for good measure none of which they could understand.

I began, "Troglodyte," "sebaceous," "wen," "helot," "indeciduity," "murine," "bantling," "ubiquity," "clithrophobia," "nadir," and instead of adding two for good measure I added seven to make their debacle more horrible. And with a pencil against the office facade I wrote the seven words so that everyone might see their eternal defeat, "abettor," "caballine," "phlebotomy," "coeval," "octroon," "risible," "anorexia," "arable," then to complete, I added, "asininity." The defeat of these educated youths was, is and will be an eternal one, because there is no other pick and shovel man that can face them like that.

From the day of that triumph they nicknamed me "solution," and we all became good friends.

And so the months passed, with plenty of joking and foolishness and no end of work.

But at times I would stand in front of the box car on a clear night. Around would be the confusion, whistles, flashes and grinding sounds of the never-ending movement in the yard. I would steal a glance up at the stars. The stars have always been the wonder of my life. I had but lately learned, to my utter surprise, that there were other worlds besides this earth. And I had also discovered in a newspaper article that the stars were other suns with unseen worlds around them. And as I gazed upward I thought that perhaps there were other eyes in those viewless worlds that were gazing wondering in my direction. And how our glances must have met in the black mid-darkness of the infinite.

Such reveries were always broken by a rough shout from some of my fellow laborers to "come in and go to sleep!"

CHAPTER XIII

During the summer of 1919 I began to hear much about *Aïda,* but I did not know exactly what it was. Federico up on Hudson Heights had been to see it; but he was unable to tell me much about it except that there was a fine parade in it.

About the same time I happened to glance over an Italian newspaper and saw an advertisement that this opera was to be represented in the open air at the Sheepshead Bay race track. I decided to go and hear it. I went there by asking my way right and left, for I knew nothing about the intricacies of Brooklyn.

And there in the middle of the confusion that attended the performance, I succeeded in worming my way to a seat right next to the orchestra, where my ears were eloquently feasted.

And all at once I felt myself being driven toward a goal. For there was revealed to me beauty, which I had been instinctively following, in spite of my grotesque jokes and farces. The quality of beauty that is in *Aïda* I have found only in the best of Shelley and perhaps Keats. There were parts of such overwhelming loveliness that they tore my soul apart. At times, afterwards, when on the job amid the confusion of running engines, car screams, and all kinds of bad noises, I heard those supreme melodies around me. I felt the impulse to rush home to our box car and compose another *Aïda*, even though I did not know one note from another, as I still don't know. And music, which I adore, is a language I have yet to learn.

About that time some of the men who lived in the box car left for Italy, and the others went to more lucrative jobs in the nearby factories. The Mexicans had all left a few months before, and as a consequence, I found myself alone in the box car with my dictionary, papers, six overcoats, a stove, two beds and a collection of broken pots.

During the general shake-up a new foreman was hired, and he came to live in a more substantially built shed next to the box car. This new foreman was a short noisy person with small black eyes and a round face. We had many good-natured arguments, and at times, starting with jests, we almost ended with blows.

In the evenings when the shadows of the Palisades had swept past us, we would sit in front of our strongholds and say bad things about each other. Then he would go off to court loudly a young lady some of whose relatives gave him a good beating shortly afterwards. And I would dig up my precious papers and dictionaries and write. At times, when he was ready to go, along would come somebody to shout that there was a wreck in the tunnel or down the lines toward the factories. And then we would hunt as many of the gang as possible and start working. Or sometimes I would be alone writing when the calamitous news would come. And then if it was very bad weather I would tell them where to find the foreman and make my escape up River Road.

During this time I was very anxious to write an opera, as I still am. The only trouble was my ignorance of music. All I could do was to take the ferry across and walk through New York often in the evenings and on Sundays, flushed, and wondering what I should do.

One fine Sunday afternoon I happened to see a sign in front of a building saying that there was a music school upstairs where they taught harmony and counterpoint. So I went up. The door was closed and I came down slowly. A man was standing in the hallway, Hibernian of features.

"The music school is closed, I suppose?" I began.

"It certainly is," he answered. "What do you want? I work there."

I asked him how much they charged, but he didn't know. Then I asked how long they took to teach music, and still he didn't know. Finally, in desperation, I asked him if he had heard of *Aïda*. "I've heard of it," he said hesitatingly, "but you should go to see the *Bohemian Girl*.

After a while I took leave of him and walked along. There was another smaller sign in front of a private house a few blocks away and I went up and rang the bell. A lady came to the door, opened her eyes in horror and almost fainted on seeing me. And I believe I must have looked very ferocious, for my suit was quite torn, my shirt dirty, I was collarless, and my shoes were falling apart. Then a man came to the door whom, I presumed, was the teacher.

"Good morning," said I, "Do you teach harmony?"

"No."

"But," I insisted, "your sign says you do."

"Perhaps," he said sharply, "What music do you know?"

"Nothing," I said ruefully.

"Well, my good fellow, you'd better learn music before trying to take up harmony."

"How can I? What must I do?" I asked in despair.

"Learn some instrument – the piano," and he slammed the door in my face.

After this rebuff I lost a good deal of my ardor for almost two hours. Then, passing a pawnshop I saw an honest-looking mandolin for sale in the window. I went in and haggled with the old man until he gave it to me for two dollars. And home I brought my trophy in triumph.

Thereafter at all sorts of uncanny hours one could hear weird plucking sounds coming from my box car. I was anxious to learn, and I also bought one of those short roads to melody which teach you to butcher some poor music by following a series of numbers. So, night and day, whenever I had time, and when by all rights I should have been sleeping, I was at my mandolin, annoying the atmosphere. I also annoyed someone else besides the clear Jersey air.

After the first few nights of music, the foreman's

small black eyes would narrow cunningly as he looked at me. And by the end of the fourth day he accused me point-blank of conjuring to destroy his sleep and drive him into a madhouse. All that evening I had been struggling with a hapless melody from *Il Trovatore*. I hadn't even thought of him, and I was surprised both at his accusation and at his ignorance of music. And I told him so.

After a few more days and arguments, he began to look very malignantly at me, and I began to watch out for trouble. Finally, a week passed, and then another. I am sure he would have fired me, had he dared. But he was a new man in the yard. And he also knew that practically everybody in the yard office was a friend of mine. So he let things drift along.

On the third Sunday he came and knocked at the door of the box car.

"What do you want?" I shouted.

"I want to speak to you just a minute."

I opened the door slowly, ready for an attack. The foreman stood outside in the sunshine smiling broadly.

"Hello," he said softly, "I want to ask a favor of you."

"What?"

"That's a fine mandolin you have," he began. "How much do you want for it?"

"It's a good mandolin," I said, stepping back, "and cheap for five dollars."

His eyes twinkled. "They surely robbed you when you paid one dollar and fifty for it."

I was justly shocked and grieved at his slight of my mandolin. And after several compromises in prices I sold it to him for three dollars and fifty cents. I was elated and he was smiling strangely. He handed over the money and I gave him the instrument.

Quickly the foreman brushed his fingers across the strings. Then with a good swing he smashed the mandolin against the door of my box car. I was surprised.

"Now I can enjoy at least one Sunday in peace," he remarked dryly as he walked into his shack. But his peace was costly, especially as I went and bought a guitar with the money.

After a while I gave up music as being an impossible job, and turned my spare moments toward literature.

And I wrote and wrote. At the same time I wrote many "poems" to my beloved of the saloon, or rather to an idealization of her, and she always served me with larger sandwiches and fuller glasses of beer. At night several of my fellow-workers would gather there and read a newspaper and discuss the woes of the world. Occasionally, still dazed from my "poetry," I would drop in, pat the cat, smile at the girl and argue with some one or other.

I once asked a few of my brighter fellow-workers if they cared to read something that sounded like the following poem: which was afterwards printed in *The Bookman:*

SONG OF LIGHT

The sun robed with noons stands on the pulpit of
    heaven
Like an anchorite preaching his faith of light to
    listening space.
And I am one of the sun's lost words,
A ray that pierces through endless emptiness on
    emptiness
Seeking in vain to be freed of its burden of
    splendor.
I was strangely surprised by their unanimous
    approval.

CHAPTER XIV

I cannot think of the old box car without a feeling
of regret. It was a wonderful place for studying the
ways of insects. Whenever it rained, water streamed
in on all sides. But it was cosy; we had a fine big
stove and plenty of coal which we picked up from
the ground after quitting time.

New men were hired; some merry old fellows
came to live in the box car. Life had taken on a
lively aspect. Yet I was dissatisfied. For I had been
thrilled by a new discovery – my senses were all
atremble – I had found Shelley.

I had already learned that there was a public library nearby in Edgewater. Going there, I was kindly
received in spite of my broken English and the ragged
appearance of my working clothes. And it was there
that, while browsing among books, I finally wandered upon "Prometheus Unbound." In a flash I recognized an appealing kinship between the climaxes
of *Aïda* and the luminous flights of that divine poetry.

Again I felt an urge to express myself, to cry out
my hopes and dreams to this lovely unheeding
world. Music was impossible for me; but Shelley I
could proceed to emulate almost immediately. As
soon as I returned to the box car I burned almost

everything I had written up to that time. Jokes, disjointed scenes and humorous "poems" all went into the cleansing flame.

I had an enormous knowledge of disjointed words and phrases and my mind was filled with fantastic impressions of life. It was hard for me to put my words and thoughts in order. Grammar gave me plenty of trouble. Rhyme stumped me. Avidly I read all kinds of poetry, during my spare time, and discovered that rhyme was not absolutely essential to poetic utterance. I also discovered, very early in my career, that a good deal of what goes under the name of poetry is really trash. So from the first I tried to avoid echoing the things I had read, and be on the safe side.

Meanwhile I became the cause of considerable argument among my fellow-workers. Some maintained that my knowledge of English would help me to advance in this world and others insisted that a man who was born a laborer could never rise. The most hopeful among them would predict that I might succeed – eventually becoming a foreman! I wonder what they would have thought had they known that I was slowly but surely deciding upon a literary career!

One of the newer men in my gang, Felice, an old man who had been strong in his youth but was now a physical wreck, told me one day:

"Pascal, what hope is there for any laborer in this world? Look at me: besides being an illiterate, I am as you see me. I walk like a duck; with a deformed hunchback for which one night I was nearly shot between the grain and chemical cars because in the dark one of the new yard watchmen thought I was taking away some valuable thing on my back. My hands are twisted and couldn't even write an "O" with a table glass. And you, who they say can write English – what good does it do you to know the language of America while working here? You are not getting a cent more than a parrot like me who goes wherever they take him. You live in the same box car. You eat the same food. And if you stay here long enough you will become the same as I. Look at me and you are looking into the mirror of your future!"

I nodded gravely.

Old Felice continued, "You should get a job in some office where you can use your English and you can learn more. Think it over, boy."

In a rose flush of awakened hopes I dreamed of my poetry. I thought of my ambition to write – always to write. It must have been a mania with me. Just at that time I had written a rough draft of a poem whose completed form was later printed in a leading magazine:

In the dark verdure of summer
The railroad tracks are like the chords of a lyre
gleaming across the dreamy valley,
And the road crosses them like a flash of lightning.
But the souls of many who speed like music on the
melodious heart-strings of the valley

Are dim with storms;
And the soul of a farm lad who plods, whistling, on
    the lightning road
Is a bright blue sky.

My awakened hopes ran high. I grew restless on the
job. I began to make mistakes, restive and annoyed
at the chains of physical labor around my new-born
soul. The realization of life had dawned upon me
with a startling suddenness.

It was on a November morning in 1919 that I
made a hasty decision. It was a quick, yet inevitable
decision. I would give my future a chance. I would
no longer dream and hope – I would act. Hurriedly
eager to execute my plans before I should change
my mind, I went to my friend Saverio.

"Saverio," I announced, "I am going to leave this
place. I am going to live in the city and write poetry."

"Pascal," he commented, "you will starve."

"I shall."

I reflected: what was one little starvation more
or less in a man's life, especially in that of a self-
anointed poet? Within an few years we would be
gone, so why not sing our songs in the meanwhile?

My friend looked sadly at me and slowly shook
his head, making me understand that we of the un-
educated class have more relations to swine and
should therefore keep on nuzzling the ground without raising our heads to cast wistful glances toward
unwritten beauties.

The next morning, oblivious of the trials ahead

of me, I came to New York with my tumble down valise in which were being transported my shirts, books and a cosmopolitan colony of insects gathered from the various corners of the vast Americas. With little misgivings I turned my back to the ditches and tracks in order to explore a new life.

When I first arrived in America the city through which I had passed had been a vast dream whirrling around me. Gradually it had taken shape and form, but had still remained alien to me in spirit. Now, however, as I walked through its crowded streets, I felt a sort of kinship with it. I felt that I was an integral part of this tremendous, living, bustling metropolis.

For several days I wandered about, getting better acquainted with my chosen abode. I felt happy. I had hopes for the future, I had a sort of goal, however vaguely defined. "Nothing," I swore to myself over and over again, "will turn me back from my chosen career of author, nothing will drive me back before I have accomplished something that will justify my starting."

So, wandering through the metropolis, I drifted down to the slums along the Brooklyn waterfront. There I could cut my expenses to a minimum. I took stock of my earthly possessions, and realized that I was in no position to stand a long period of physical idleness. In the first impetus of enthusiasm, however, I wrote continuously for several weeks. It seemed to be a great relief to have all my time free for my beloved poetry.

After a few weeks in this great metropolis I wrote a poem called "The City":

> We who were born through the love of God must
>   die through the hatred of Man.
> We who grapple with the destruction of ignorance
>   and the creation of unwitting love –
> We struggle, blinded by dismal night in a weird
>   shadowy city.
> Yet the city itself is lifting street-lamps, like a
>   million cups filled with light,
> To quench from the upraised eyes their thirst of
>   gloom;
> And from the hecatombs of aching souls
> The factory smoke is unfolding in protesting curves
> Like phantoms of black unappeased desires,
>   yearning and struggling and pointing upward;
> While through its dark streets pass people, tired,
>   useless,
> Trampling the vague black illusions
> That pave their paths like broad leaves of water-
>   lilies
> On twilight streams;
> And there are smiles at times on their lips.
> Only the great soul, denuded to the blasts of reality,
> Shivers and groans.
> And like two wild ideas lost in a forest of thoughts,
> Blind hatred and blinder love run amuck through
>   the city.

I took this poem and several others which I had culled from my growing collection and sent them to a magazine which sometimes allows the muses a few odd corners. This was my first bombardment upon

the editorial citadels. And my success was rather assured for I had put two stamps upon the envelope
with heads of Washington on them. And if one Washington had been such a valiant warrior, I thought in
jest, then, two should practically overwhelm the editorial fortresses. Thus did I play in this toy city amid
the vigilant realities of this toy universe.

Thereafter, every evening, on coming home I
guided my steps toward my landlord's dingy room
to ask if any letter had come for me. As an answer
he would shake his head.

So continuous and anxious were my inquiries
about the letter that he concluded it must be something of great value. Therefore when the small, but
robust letter came he was tempted to investigate.

Disappointed, and more than a little indignant,
at not having found any of the earth's material
wealth in it, the landlord brought the letter to me,
"Here you are, sir, I hope it's what you were expecting."

I thanked him and rushed to my room. No
sooner had I lit the kerosene lamp than I began to
search the letter for money or for an invitation to
call at the editor's office. Instead I found my poems and a printed slip. It was elaborate and diplo-
matic, courteously thanking me for my kindness in
allowing the editorial staff to consider my poems.
I was flattered. I was pleased to think that the editors of a large and opulent magazine should thank
me.

Immediately I procured two more envelopes,

filled them with poems and sent them out. Without hesitation they were sent back accompanied by printed slips. Those editors must have strongly believed in accuracy and promptness. This encouraged me to send out more and soon my collection of courteous slips had grown to large proportions, since I had begun to invade other redoubts.

Gradually I became skeptical about the honeyed phrases. I strongly suspected that there was some telepathic communication among the magazine editors to drive me and my poems from the thresholds of their temples.

And now I realized that I was merely a small drop in the sad whirlpool of literary aspirants. In my cold, stoveless, dingy room or in the Library, I was alone in my struggle to acquire a new language and a new world. But outside of that I was one, only one of the millions of literary beggars who clog the halls of literature, who stand like a sluggish crowd in the way of anyone wishing to forge ahead.

For a while I became discouraged utterly. Everyone is in everyone else's way, I thought. There are too many authors, too many poets, novelists, dramatists, too many people honestly yearning to speak their souls, and this commercial world cannot assimilate them all.

I went back to work. I found a job in a wild, insane shipyard nearby. I was restless. I tried to forget poetry, I tried to forget beauty. I tried to lead the drab, hard life which it seems fate had allotted to me. Days passed, and still I toiled. The weeks and

then the months passed. With a sort of feverish anger I shook my head at the thought of a literary
career, in spite of all that I had said before. But the
Enchantress would not let me free. I was restless.
Something appeared to be lacking in my life. At night
when I should have been sleeping I would sit up and
struggle with my own indecisions. My only refuge
from my hounding feverish thoughts was toil – hard,
ceaseless, life-sapping toil. I rarely spoke to anyone
save on the job.

The winter of 1920 passed and Spring flew by in
a blaze of soul-torture. It was hard for me to com-
bat the spell of beauty. It was hard for me to think
that I could never succeed.

One evening late that summer, while wandering
aimlessly around I happened to pick up a copy of a
staid and respectable metropolitan newspaper. On
the editorial page was a poem which struck me as
being the most blatant and silly trash imaginable.
Immediately a suggestive fury blazed in me. My
thoughts roared all aflame, "How is it that such
stuff is printed while I must go pleading in vain from
door to door?"

"Perseverance!" answered my own mind, "Perseverance! you cannot succeed by slinking away from
the fight. Keep it up! If such trash is printed, then
there is hope for your writing."

All at once I had to burst out laughing. The poet
– a lady – had most probably hounded the editors
until in desperation they had accepted her effusions.
Good! Then I would hound them too!

Decided, encouraged, I went home and cutting out the poem pasted it on my door to be forever before me as the "horrible example."

The next day I quit my job. From now on there was to be no turning back. I would acknowledge no defeat.

Timidly I went to an Italian newspaper, hoping that I might find some encouragement there from people of my own blood.

The editor read my poems and commented, "We only print works of well-known writers. We cannot do anything for you."

"Why," I pleaded, "some American newspapers pay from $5 to $10; but I ask no price. You can give as much as you please."

"Ten dollars! We wouldn't give you even ten cents," he replied.

I went to other publications and received similar receptions. I sent poems to magazines in other cities and received the inevitable printed slips. One editor did deign to write something on the slip and that was a note to please send a self-addressed stamped envelope with my contributions.

It took courage to continue writing in those months, but I kept it up. I forced myself to believe in eventual success. Whenever I felt weakening I would read the poem pasted on the door.

The winter of 1921 was approaching. Times were bad. Recognition seemed utterly impossible, in spite of my set resolve. A literary future for me was the densest, sunless, moonless, starless gloom the human mind could ever conceive. How far would my scanty savings of the preceding months take me?

I tried to save money in all ways possible. I went to live in the cheapest hole that I could find in the slums of Brooklyn. It was a small room which had previously been a chicken coop and wood shack. That hovel was the main tryst where all the most undesirable inconveniences held their meetings. The entrance to it was through a toilet which served ten families besides unwelcome strangers and dirty passers-by. Often the overflow of that ordure would come running beneath the door and stand in malodorous pools under my bug-infested bed.

There was no stove in the room, and many a freezing day I had to remain huddled in the bed in order to keep warm. The most dyspeptic and indigestible moments were those when I had to shave. I could scarcely shave with my overcoat on – which served me as a quilt at night and as an overcoat during the day.

All those who knew where I was living could hardly refrain from saying, "Are you crazy to live in that room without a stove and toilet water always coming in? You will easily get sick."

I shrugged my shoulders in resignation and tried to make them understand that the price of a better room was beyond my financial compass.

Meanwhile I would go to the Library – the only refuge opened to me – and write. At least if my body was living in a world of horror I could build a world of beauty for my soul.

Having little money left I set out to master the situation. The easiest thing to cut was food. I searched every possible corner for cheap food. I went into several bakeries and asked for the lowest price on their bread. Too high – too high – always too high. But my search continued. I went into one place and asked the same question. The lady there told me, adding, "Unless you want stale bread." I smiled and jested solemnly, "How much must I disburse for your stale bread before I can proclaim it mine?"

Open-mouthed she stared at me, though she understood "how much." And I became a steady customer for stale bread, although very often I would call it "steel bread" which really was an appropriate name.

Poverty, the eternal torturer, tightened its hold upon me. As days of hopeless darkness followed each other I felt myself constrained to cut down expenses in all possible ways. It was a war for an ideal. For my part I began to live on the most frugal basis imaginable. My daily meals during that winter consisted of stale bread and cold soup in which I put stale bread broken into small pieces and waited until they became soft enough to be eaten, costing, in all, about ten cents. At times I would get reckless and squander a few pennies for bananas – if I could get them cheap enough.

Do not think that I bought those finely assorted bananas with which the corner fruit stands so allure the passer-by. Not by any means. Those which I ate – delicious food – were sold to me, not one cent each, but twenty-five, and sometimes even more, for a nickel. These were not daily occurrences, only Saturdays made them possible. One can easily imagine in what state of decomposition they were to fetch such a low price. For me, in my struggle against poverty, they were a rare delicacy. A banana vendor once, the first time I approached his stand, asked me, "Are you buyin' this bananas for your dog?"

"No," I replied promptly, "for my 'wolf.'"

Several times on my way home with soup I would begin to tremble – and there was a good reason for it – for if the Prohibition agents ever inspected my soup they would arrest me. Because my soup, in its state of fermentation, would far surpass their constitutionalized one-half of one per cent. Sometimes besides being sour and burnt – at times so badly damaged that I had to throw it away and bemoan the nickel which I had lost in that bad investment – my soup was full of bones – bones that did not belong there. Meatless bones, chicken feet which were dead, but alive enough to scratch my soul with deep humiliation. But the more things turned against me, the more I stood my ground.

I had faith in myself. Without realizing it, I had learned the great lesson of America: I had learned to have faith in the future. No matter how bad things were, a turn would inevitably come – as long as I did not give up. I was sure of it. But how much I had to suffer until the change came! What a thorny, heartbreaking road it was!

CHAPTER XV

As the winter grew more severe my condition became desperate. My books and papers were moulding from the damp. I too felt that I was mouldering. The sufferings, colds, wet and damp were beginning to harm me. Many a freezing night, unable to remain in bed I had to get up and walk about three miles to the Long Island Depot at Flatbush Avenue where I might find a little warmth.

Once I had to stay three days without washing because the lavatory pipes were frozen. On the morning of the fourth day I thought it was worthwhile going to the Main Library at Forty-second Street and Fifth Avenue where I could wash not only my hands and face but my handkerchief also.

I took some stale bread with me and five or six bananas, because that was all I had left. Wrapping the remainder of the bread, destined to last at least two more days, in a sheet of newspaper; I threw it under the bed. Usually, on going out, I would place my bread in the bed rather than under, fearing lest the unwelcome toilet overflows would pay a visit during my absence and render it uneatable. But now that the pipes were frozen I needed no such precautions.

While I was in the public library, several hours later, I had occasion to go from the main reading room to see about a book in the files outside. During my absence some conscientious gentleman inspected my overcoat which I had left on the arm of my chair believing that the library was only frequented by honest people.

Finding it too old to repay him for the trouble of taking it away, he searched the pockets and took the few pennies that I had left.

I was unaware of this until I was approaching the subway station, when my hand instinctively began to feel for the fare.

The lady in the booth – though I did not ask her for anything – made me understand that the B. R. T. was not a philanthropic society.

I turned away from the booth and went up to the street.

Without wasting more time I set out on my long tramp home. It was about half-past ten when I left Times Square. The weather was somewhat cloudy, though I could see no visible signs of either snow or frozen rain.

"It is not so bad after all," I thought, "especially if it does not snow." By two o'clock I ought to be in my hovel. Why did I try to go in the subway, anyhow? Why was I in such a hurry to reach my room? Was there a woman's brightening smile and a child's love-woven da! da! to greet me after their alarm on account of my delay? What was there home for me? Only cold and overflows. Well, they could overflow without me.

I walked.

The wind began to make itself more arrogant. As I was about to reach Canal Street some cold sharp rain began to fall from the sluggish clouds, with increasing rapidity.

Just as I was in the middle of Manhattan Bridge the rain and sleet began to pour full blast upon the city. My face ached from the sharp biting sleet. Two minutes were sufficient to get me wet through to the skin. My clothes became bright and studded with the frozen rain. I could not pause for if I did my water soaked underwear would freeze me. I hurried on head-bowed.

Reaching the Long Island Depot on Flatbush Avenue I entered in order to warm myself a little. I stood there shivering in my cold wet clothes.

Snow could be seen through the glass windows pouring down as intense as the clouds above that threw it.

It was about one A.M. Besides feeling cold and extremely wet, I was hungry. I could not go into a restaurant. I did not have a cent. Neither could I eat snow.

After a while I hurried home under the piercing blows of the ice-pointed wind. There at least I had my stale bread under the bed. It was home after all.

I reached my room a little after two. As I opened the door in the dark I could hear a splashing on the floor as if water were there. The window was open. Snow poured in. The children of the neighborhood had opened it during my absence in order to look at my books and papers. Rain and snow had wet a good half of the bed and quilt. Someone had also tried to warm the pipes in the lavatory and they had burst. Before the water could be turned off enough of it had flowed under my bed to spoil my stale bread and my extra pair of trousers and underwear.

Half of my bed was wet. I could not use it. My underwear was also soaked. The stale bread gave such an evil toilet smell that I could not eat it in spite of my hunger. Shivering, sleepy, hungry, tired, I huddled on the dry end of the bed and pressed my face in anguish against the quilt. How long, O God, how long was this going to last? Would I ever get out of this gulf of sorrows?

I must have fallen asleep, for just as the gray tumult outside was whitening into dawn, I awoke aching and coughing, with fits of fever. I did not feel myself able to plunge through the snowdrifts that filled the streets and so sat shivering in my room while the day cleared and an icy wind blew against my window.

What an immense distance stretched between me and my goal! What an impossibility it appeared to see even one word of mine in print!

Somehow, the sufferings and discouragements which I received during those terrible months only spurred me to greater efforts. Systematically, I made a list of all the newspapers and magazines in New York. And I decided to pay personal visits to all of them. I selected about a score of my poems and divided them into four equal groups so that I could cover several offices in one day. My visits to the newspapers proved useless and discouraging. Some made me leave the poems, saying, "You will hear from us soon," though three or four weeks usually passed before the unfavorable news came. One newspaper, out of pity, I suppose, offered me a dollar for my favorite poems.

Late in December, while the happy populace were beginning their festive squandering, I went to the office of a large, internationally known newspaper. Downcast and sad, I sat on a chair in the receiving room waiting for someone to come and reject my poems. All at once a young man who was passing, stopped abruptly and opened his eyes with amazement at my queer presence.

I rose to my feet and gazed pleadingly at him.

"What's the matter, are you sick?" he asked in a semi-jesting voice.

"No, though I have some poems that are from lack of recognition."

A sardonic grin passed over his face at the mention of "poems." "Well, you are in the wrong hospital then, John," he said, walking on.

After a minute or two a solemn looking gentleman came out to lend dignity and weight to the antechamber.

"What can I do for you?" he inquired as if he were the doctor sent out to feel the pulse of my poems. I showed him my poems.

"I am very sorry, sir," he began austerely, "but I can do nothing for you. Our policy, or rather the policy of this paper does not enable us to print anything except what is written by our editorial staff. I wish you luck. Good-bye."

Similar receptions did not deter me. There was always the goading thought that if ninety-nine offices rejected my poems the hundredth might accept them.

When I went home at night, there was nothing to cheer me in the freezing, stoveless room, save the encouraging thought that I had not yet visited all the editorial offices in New York. Why then should I buy the coffin before my hope was dead? At times, seized by fits of enthusiasm, about an imaginary success, I would sit down and write, forgetting hunger and cold which beset me.

Toward the end of the year I went into a magazine office from which my poems had been twice expelled and asked the information girl if I could see the editor. I wanted to make sure that it was the editor and not the office boy who had read my poems.

"I am not sure, but I'll try," she said.

After a while I was brought into the presence of a quiet looking old gentleman around whose eyes there seemed to be a touch of sadness.

In a voice whose harshness startled me, coming as it did from such a mild looking man, he asked, "Well, what brought you here?"

I told him that I had come to ask about my poems. His office had held them for such a long time that I had almost begun to hope for their ultimate acceptance, and then they had been suddenly returned to me.

"To tell the truth," he began, "I am editor, and the poems which we print are selected by a special reader out of the large quantity that pours into our office. Therefore you can easily understand that I have in no wise ever seen yours or anybody else's poems except those which the reader hands to me for the magazine. And that is about all I have to say. Good day."

Such receptions were repeated over and over again with sickening monotony. And still I persisted.

During the time I was working in the Under-cliff yard of the Erie I had written a poem called "Light" which summed up my indecisions and doubts about the future. And the light had not yet come.

LIGHT

Every morning, while hurrying along River Road to
     work,
I pass the old miser Stemowski's hut,
Beside which pants a white perfumed cloud of
     acacias.
And the poignant spring pierces me.
My eyes are suddenly glad, like cloud-shadows
     when they meet the sheltering gloom
After having been long stranded in a sea of glassy
     light.
Then I rush to the yard.
But on the job my mind still wanders along the
     steps of dreams in search of beauty.
O how I bleed in anguish! I suffer
Amid my happy, laughing but senseless toilers!

Perhaps it is the price of a forbidden dream sunken
in the purple sea of an obscure future.

Toward the end of the year, as one of the last few
hopes, I submitted my poems in a contest which
The Nation was holding. It was a desperate move, a
clutching at a straw.

The year ended and no answer came. I became
anxious; I wanted to know what had befallen my
poems. I knew that recognition was practically impossible. It was a new year of sorrow and suffering.
As a sort of despairing gesture I sent a letter to the
editor.

> *To the Editor of* The Nation,
> *Dear Sir:*
> *I have submitted three poems "For* The Nation's
> *Poetry Prize" within the established period as de-
> scribed in the columns of* The Nation! *Not having
> heard anything from your editorial office, I would
> be much obliged if you should inform me on the
> matter.*
>
> *I hope you will consider them from a viewpoint
> of their having been written by one who is an igno-
> rant pick and shovel man – who has never studied
> English. If they do not contain too many mistakes I
> must warmly thank those friends who have been kind
> enough to point out the grammatical errors. I am one
> who is struggling through the blinding flames of ig-
> norance to bring his message before the public – be-
> fore you. You are dedicated to defend the immense
> cause of the oppressed. This letter is the cry of a soul
> stranded on the shores of darkness looking for light –*

a light that points out the path toward recognition, where I can work and help myself. I am not deserting the legions of toil to refuge myself in the literary world. No! No! I only want to express the wrath of their mistreatment. No! I seek no refuge! I am a worker, a pick and shovel man – what I want is an outlet to express what I can say besides work. Yes to express all the sorrows of those who cower under the crushing yoke of an unjust doom.

There are no words that can fitly represent my living sufferings. No, no words! Even the picture loses its mute eloquence before this scene. I suffer: for an ideal, for freedom, for truth that is denied by millions, but not by the souls who have the responsibility of being human. For yesterday, New Year's Day, I only had five cents worth of decaying bananas and a loaf of stale bread to eat. And today: a half quart of milk and a stale loaf of bread. All for the love of an ideal. Not having sufficient bed clothes for a stoveless room like mine, I must use my overcoat as blanket at night and as a wrinkled overcoat during the day. The room is damp – my books are becoming mouldered. And I too am beginning to feel the effects of it. But what can I do? Without a pick and shovel job and without a just recognition. And besides the landlady has notified me to evacuate her room on or before January the tenth. She may have someone who can pay a little more than I. So I must go and search for another room. Perhaps it will cost more than this. How can I afford it? Without work and without a recognition that will allow me to work?

Please consider my condition and the quality of the work I submit. Then say if I can be helped without any expense on your part. You can do – do something for me. Even in this horrible and indescribable condition I am not asking for financial aid. I am not asking for pity, nor am I asking for an impossibility. I only ask for a simple thing – a thing which you are giving away free. While you are giving it away free, why not see that it goes where it can help the most? I am not coveting the prize because of the money. No but because it will give me the recognition that I cannot do without. If it's given to me I can go around to all the editors, and I can say to them that I have been awarded "The Nation's Poetry Prize." When I say that, they will listen to me – they will consider my works – they will begin to accept them. Then, dominated by an impulse of encouragement, I will write: a novel, two, three, who knows how many! But how can I go now without an introduction of this kind? They don't hear me. If I ask them to see my manuscript they say they are busy, or else they let me leave some poems which they put hatching oblivion, in an obscure corner of their editorialocratic drawers. When after a certain time they might accidentally happen to see my poems they glance at the name and see it's an unknown one. Therefore they return them without much consideration. Must it continue like this forever? That is why I am asking this help from you. If it is a help without expenses then why not help me? If the prize is given to a well known writer it does not give him the same aid that it gives me.

There is no writer who exists under such conditions. Let this prize break those horrible barriers before me, and open a new world of hope! Let this prize (even if it is an honorary one) come like a bridge of light between me and my awaiting future. Let me free! Let me free! Free like the thought of love that haunts millions of minds. If it's without expenses on your side then, give, give me an opportunity. Give me an opportunity before colds, wet, sleets, and many other sufferings will pitilessly distort my physical and mental shapes into a monstrous deformity. Give me an opportunity while it's not too late. I can work hard and am hoping to make enough money to have a musical education. For I want to compose music. And yet I do not know the difference between one note and another. What bars me from doing so?

Oh! Please hear me! I am telling the truth. And yet who knows it? Only I. And who believes me? Then let my soul break out of the chrysalis of enforced ignorance and fly toward the flower of hope, like a rich butterfly winged with a thousand thoughts of beauty.

Remember! without any expenses on your side you can help me! This is what I want: to be one sharer (though honorary) of the prize, the honor of the prize, a winner of the prize! For I have no friends who can help me in the literary world. I am a poor worker but a rich defender of truth.

Oh please! The weights of duty crush me down and yet I can not perform. I am not a spendthrift. With a hundred dollars I can live five months. I am not asking an impossibility.

Lift me, with strength of the prize, out of this ignoble gloom and place me on the pulpit of light where I too can narrate what the Nature-made orator has to say in me.

The miracle happened. All at once I found myself known and talked about. Almost immediately my plea found a sympathetic response and the two editors of two influential weekly publications in America became interested in my work. Henry Seidel Canby, editor of *The Literary Review* of the *New York Evening Post,* was one of them. Poems of mine were published. Other magazines followed. Soon the newspapers began to print my story and word about me appeared in Europe and throughout America.

The literary world began to take me up as a great curiosity and I was literally feasted, welcomed and stared at. Letters of congratulation and appreciation came from various sections of America: from Boston to 'Frisco. But more sincere and dearer to my heart were the tributes of my fellow workers who recognized that at last one of them had risen from the ditches and quicksands of toil to speak his heart to the upper world.

And sweeter yet was the happiness of my parents who realized that after all I had not really gone astray, but had sought and attained a goal far from the deep-worn groove of peasant drudgery.

SON OF ABRUZZI

n his 1924 "Introduction" to Pascal D'Angelo's *Son
of Italy*, Carl Van Doren writes that D'Angelo's immigrant autobiography is another story about
struggle, success, and assimilation in American soci-
ty. He locates *Son of Italy* in the well-established
success story genre of the era defined by the novels
of Horatio Alger and the autobiographies of busi-
nessmen such as Andrew Carnegie and John D.
Rockefeller (Huber). A Columbia University profes-
sor and one of the most preeminent literary critics
of the 1920s, Van Doren informed his readers that
this was a "pick and shovel" narrative about "enormous hardships," "struggles," "disadvantages," and
"chance." Van Doren wrote that it "excels all others
in the type of which his book is an example."

However, Van Doren's simplistic view of *Son of
Italy* obscures the immigrant D'Angelo's real struggle
with the process of assimilation in his narrative. In
fact, D'Angelo's narrative is a countertext to the
melting pot theory that dominated American soci-
ty at the time. Constantine Panunzio wrote in his
1921 autobiography, *The Soul of an Immigrant*, with
the end of World War I American society "turned its
attention to the all-important question of the assimilation of the immigrant . . ." In response to the

discourse over assimilation at the time, D'Angelo does encode in his narrative that widely-recognized image of the struggling individual required by the success genre. But throughout the narrative, the ethnic voice that speaks undermines the image of the successful, assimilated self and any attempts to read *Son of Italy* as a unitary, immigrant success story.

D'Angelo's style is the first indication of the complexity of the narrative's message. Throughout, in both the poetry and prose, the narrative style reflects the historical D'Angelo's unsuccessful struggle to locate the subaltern immigrant self in the language of upper-class literary culture. In his quest for self-improvement, the historical D'Angelo supposedly learns English and discovers high culture in the poetry of Shelley and Keats and in Italian opera. Under the influence of his limited exposure to high culture, D'Angelo locates the narrative at crucial junctures in what he mistakenly perceives to be formal literary language (Leibowitz). At these places in the text it becomes clear that D'Angelo attempts to speak in a language not his own, linguistically, socially, and culturally. D'Angelo's style in both the poems and certain sections of the prose narrative is often embellished with extended metaphors, personification, and inappropriate adjectives. In the first sentence of the *Son of Italy* D'Angelo writes, "As I glance back over the time-shrouded sky of my infancy, I see a vast expanse of mist that gives no light to any early events." In a poem entitled "The City," he intones, "And like two wild ideas lost in a forest of thoughts, / Blind hatred and blinder love run amuck through the city." In the most formal trope of all, he entitles another poem, *"Omnis Sum,"* though he admits to having little facility in Italian, let alone Latin.

Likewise, in another appeal to literary convention in his narrative, he locates his boyhood self in that familiar, idealized Old World setting made popular at the time by British writers such as George Gissing and Norman Douglas and the famous American romance writer Francis Marion Crawford (Pilkington 103-118). He writes that his village lies under the shadow of the mythical Mt. Majella and is in the vicinity of ancient Italic sites, including a garden purportedly dedicated to Ovid. More important, he tells a seemingly harmless folkloric tale about superstitious peasants and a village woman, an acknowledged "vampire," who is accused of casting a spell on a village boy and causing his death. D'Angelo describes the "vampire" in the typically picturesque language of the genre: the "old hag" is "ugly," and "shrunken," but her eyes have "a strange majesty." Because of her malevolent powers, she is driven from the village and later killed by the boy's father.

Left by themselves in the narrative, these episodes inhabit a seemingly ideologically neutered space in both Southern Italian culture and in the reading tastes of D'Angelo's upper-class, American audience at the time. However, a chapter later, D'Angelo undermines his conventional folkloric story with an unexpected enunciation: "It is the landowners and the money

lenders who are the real vampires among us – not
pitiable, demented old women." He unmasks the
sublimated ideological frustrations of the powerless
villagers in their murder of the old woman. He undermines the idealized folkloric tropes and relocates
them stylistically in the historical and contempo-
rary circumstances of the economic exploitation of
the colonized Southern Italian peasantry (Gramsci).

Earlier in the narrative, D'Angelo explains that
he and his family lived in a rat-infested hovel that
they shared with their farm animals. They had little
food and his father had no hope for a secure job. As
D'Angelo goes on to explain in Chapter IV, the peasants are humiliated by the *signori* of the village. The
"rich few" own all the cultivatable land and lease it
out at "usurious" rates. Peasants work for "two cents
a day," and when they lease land, they must pay
upwards to "four-fifths" of their harvest to the landlord. To survive, the peasants are forced to overwork
themselves and become "sickened with malaria" and
become "ghosts of their former selves." Ultimately,
D'Angelo's realistic descriptions of peasant life un-
dermine his idealized images of ancient Italica and
village life. The only escape from the "spectre of starvation "and their perpetual servitude was for the
fifteen-year old D'Angelo and his father to immi-
grate to that "boundless America."

From the outset of his years in America, D'Angelo
creates an irremediable contradiction in his bivocal
narrative. No matter how hard he struggles to succeed, his peasant past and immigrant status under-

mine his best efforts to assimilate into American society. When D'Angelo describes his immigrant experiences as ghetto dweller and migratory pick and shovel man in America, his mimetic style, derived from the newly won status of the realistic novel in America, contrasts radically with the formal language of the poems that he inserts throughout his text (Cady). He locates the self in the naturalistic details of subaltern urban life. To enhance the "realism" of this text, D'Angelo recalls interior monologues and dialogues, improbable recollections after the passage of so many years. (Thompson 1-20). The realistic perspective that D'Angelo brings to his narrative serves, in Mikhail Bakhtin's terms, to "dialogize" the voice in the narrative. D'Angelo's realistic style radically bifurcates the pick and shovel Italian immigrant self between the mimetic and abstract: between the pick and shovel immigrant and the intended assimilated American self that is struggling to emerge in the narrative (Bergland).

Once in America, D'Angelo replaces the peonage system of colonized Southern Italy with the Diaspora of the post-colonial immigrant experience (Verdicchio). The rift between the subaltern Southern Italian immigrant and the assimilated American only widens. For security D'Angelo and his father take refuge in the work gang, the deterritorialized family composed of seven men from Introdacqua. For the Abruzzese work gang, immigration leads to migration. In their seven years of travel and toil together, D'Angelo describes their struggle to survive

in their squalid work camps and the equally squalid
Northeastern ethnic ghettoes. In one outstanding
example, he cites a West Virginia labor camp that is
designed to perpetuate the workers' bondage in near
slavery to the company that employs them: "Everywhere was toil – continuous toil . . . " On the streets
of New York D'Angelo hears "slurring remarks about
those foreigners." To his disappointment he learns
that Americans hold prostitutes, with their "glaring
yellow hair" and "blood-red lips," in higher regard
than they do immigrants.

When D'Angelo's father, homesick and discouraged after seven years of unproductive labor, decides
to return to Italy, the work gang is dispersed. Significantly, D'Angelo does not dwell on his father's
failure to succeed. D'Angelo merely announces, "I
was left alone." The narrative "we" changes to the
narrative "I." The Abruzzese culture of the extended
"family" is replaced with the Anglophone culture
of individualism. After his father's departure, he suddenly rejects the struggle for material success in
America and decides to become a writer. D'Angelo's
ghetto experiences of "hunger," "anguish," "suffering," and "discouragement" are framed by his idealized, rhetorical tropes of "success," "faith,"
"freedom," and "perseverance." In the closing chap-
ters of his narrative, D'Angelo focuses on the image
of the impoverished immigrant struggling to be re-
constructed into the self-made man.

After years of perseverance in submitting his poems to publications and living in abject poverty, the

judicial requirements of the success story, he finally "succeeds." Van Doren, Henry Canby, the editor of *The Literary Review*, and the editors of the *New York Evening Post* finally accept some of D'Angelo's poems. But by D'Angelo's own admission, he is little more than a transitory, literary "curiosity." While in the end the autobiographical self does appear to be allowed into the Anglophile "temples," as Van Doren implies in his introduction, the reality is that the guardians of American culture ultimately relegated *Son of Italy*, in D'Angelo's terms, to the obscurity of their "editorialocratic drawers." In spite of his success, the immigrant D'Angelo insists in the end of his narrative that he remains "a worker, a pick and shovel man . . ." The opposition between that successful, American self that is struggling to emerge in the end of the text and the reality of the immigrant self is not resolved.

Given his English language skills, lack of education, and perhaps most important of all, his "race," the historical D'Angelo could never have assumed the editorships of the various American literary journals that he was supposedly offered upon his "discovery" by *The Nation*. Ironically, complicating D'Angelo's success, if not the success of all immigrants at the time, *Son of Italy* appeared the same year that Congress passed the nativist-inspired Johnson-Reed Act, intended to limit the number of Asian, Southern, and Eastern European immigrants (Hingham 322-24).

Ultimately, there was no place for immigrants in

the essentialist Italian Renaissance canon and in the curriculum of the American academy at the time. For Van Doren and his colleagues in the Anglophone American university, canonical Italy was found in the pages of Jacob Burckhardt's famous *The Civilization of the Renaissance in Italy*, an Italy located in the idealized iconography of its Renaissance art and the equally hierarchical social structure of its Renaissance city states. Significantly, in his Introduction, Van Doren never calls D'Angelo an Italian. Rather, Van Doren describes D'Angelo as a typical example "of the peasants of his race." He simultaneously relegates D'Angelo to that subaltern, Southern European "race," as well as to that picturesque Introdacqua, which only shepherds, vampires, and peasants occupy in the ideologically inscribed upper-class, American imagination of the era. Furthermore, Burckhardt's widely read study reinforced with the authority of scholarship and history two major American discourses of the 1920s. He defined the Italian Renaissance as the era "that gave the highest development to individuality," a concept central to the success genre (226). Also, his exposure of the papacy's secular powers and of the profligacy of the Church's ecclesiastical orders played equally well in the revival of anti-Catholic nativism in the aftermath of World War I (Hingham 266). Indeed, nativist sentiment at the time even accused the immigrant of importing seditious ideas into American culture as well (Fuller).

In spite of *Son of Italy's* failure as an assimilationist

narrative, it remains relevant to us today. In both his problematic style and content, D'Angelo expresses the same conflicts over history, culture, and identity that other Italian American writers of the era addressed in their narratives, from Garibaldi Lapolla, Guido D'Agostino, and Michael De Capite to Pietro Di Donato, George Panetta, and Louis Forgione, to whom D'Angelo dedicates *Son of Italy*. What these writers tell us in their narratives is that the immigrant's European identity would not be so easily shucked in America as nativists demanded and as St. Jean de Crèvecoeur or Frederick Jackson Turner imagined it would be in the New World. The unity that Henry Adams saw disintegrating at the end of the nineteenth century in *The Education* and the cultural multiplicity that Henry James observed in *The American Scene* manifest themselves in that often conflicted bivocal ethnic voice in *Son of Italy* (Boelhower).

Son of Italy went through only one edition and was never reprinted (D'Angelo). The disappearance of *Son of Italy* is evidence enough that there was no place for the immigrant self in the highbrow modernist American canon of the 1920s. No matter how hard D'Angelo struggled to become an assimilated "son of Italy," he remains "son of Abruzzi." The subaltern immigrant self, with its ideological interpretation of Italian folklore and history and its mimetic representation of the American capitalist peonage system, was anathema to the highbrow essentialism of the American literary establishment. *Son of Italy* remains an important text to us because it reveals the complex, polyvocal discourse that Italian American narratives continue to engage in with American culture in the twenty-first century.

Kenneth Scambray
University of La Verne

WORKS CITED

Bakhtin, M.M. *The Dialogic Imagination*. Ed. Michael Holquist. Trans. Caryl Emerson and Michael Holquist. Austin: University of Texas Press, 1981.

Bergland, Betty. "Postmodernism and the Autobiographical Subject: Reconstructing the 'Other,'" in *Autobiography and Postmodernism*. Ed. Kathleen Ashley, Leigh Gilmore, & Gerald Peters. Amherst: University of Massachusetts Press, 1994. 130-166.

Boelhower, William. *Immigrant Autobiography in the United States*. Verona: Essedue Edizione, 1982.

—. "The Making of Ethnic Autobiography in the United States," in *American Autobiography*. Ed., Paul John Eakin. Madison: University of Wisconsin Press, 1991. 123-141.

Burckhardt, Jacob. *The Civilization of the Renaissance in Italy*. New York: Random House, 1954.

Cady, Edwin H. *The Realist At War: The Mature Years 1885-1920 of William Dean Howells*. New York:Syracuse University Press, 1958.

Crawford, F. Marion. *The Novel: What Is It?* New York: MacMillan & Company, 1893.

D'Angelo, Pascal. *Son of Italy*. New York: The Macmillan Company, 1924.

—. *Son of Italy*. New York: Arno Press, 1975.

—. *Son of Italy*. Traduzione e note di Sonia Pendola. Introduzione di Luigi Fontanella. Salerno: Edizioni "Il Grappolo," 1999.

Douglas, Norman. *Old Calabria*. London: Martin Secker, 1915.

Fuller, Henry Blake. "The Melting Pot Begins to Smell." *New York Times Book Review* 21 Dec. 1924, p. 2. See also Szuberla, Guy. "Henry Blake Fuller and the 'New Immigrant.'" *American Literature* 53 (May 1981): 246-265.

Gissing, George. *By the Ionian Sea: Notes of a Ramble in Southern Italy*. London: Chapman and Hall Ltd., 1901.

Gramsci, Antonio. "The Southern Question." *The Modern Prince and Other Writings*. New York: International Publishers, 1975.

Higham, John. *Strangers in the Land: Patterns of American Nativism, 1860-1925*. New Brunswick: Rutgers University Press, 1988.

Huber, Richard, M. *The American Idea of Success*. New York: McGraw-Hill, 1971.

Leibowitz, Herbert, A. *Fabricating Lives: Explorations in American Autobiography*. New York: Knopf, 1989.

Panunzio, Constantine M. *The Soul of an Immigrant*. New York: The MacMillan Company, 1921.

Pilkington, John, Jr. *Francis Marion Crawford*. New York: Twayne Publishers, 1964.

Thompson, Charles P., et al. *Autobiographical Memory: Remembering What and Remembering When*. New Jersey: L. Erlbaum Associates, Pub., 1996.

Verdicchio, Pasquale. "Subalterns Abroad." *Devils in Paradise: Writings on Post-Emigrant Cultures*. Toronto: Guernica Editions, Inc. 1999. 7-26.